PLEASE HEAR WHAT I'M NOT SAYING

A Poem's Reach Around The World

For Pauline
May There be things in
here that speak to you.

Charlie Finn
January 2012

Charles C. Finn

authorHOUSE®

AuthorHouse™
1663 Liberty Drive
Bloomington, IN 47403
www.authorhouse.com
Phone: 1-800-839-8640

First published by AuthorHouse   11/18/2011

ISBN: 978-1-4678-2963-2 (sc)
ISBN: 978-1-4678-2960-1 (e)

Printed in the United States of America

Any people depicted in stock imagery provided by Thinkstock are models, and such images are being used for illustrative purposes only.
Certain stock imagery © Thinkstock.

This book is printed on acid-free paper.

To all who have made this book possible
by sharing their heartfelt responses
to a message found in a bottle.

Table of Contents

I Want to Write Something So Simply

I want to write something
so simply
about love
or about pain
that even
as you are reading
you feel it
and as you read
you keep feeling it
and though it be my story
it will be common,
though it be singular
it will be known to you
so that by the end
you will think—
no, you will realize—
that it was all the while
yourself arranging the words,
that it was all the time
words that you yourself,
out of your own heart
had been saying.

(from Mary Oliver's *Evidence)*

Prologue

Standing at that magical place where sand meets sea, you likely have imagined putting a message in a bottle, consigning it to the waves, hoping it might some day reach another shore, and then not only be read but, incredibly across space and time, make a difference in other lives now connected to your own. It has happened to me, and I must sing of it.

In the autumn of 1966 I let the waves carry off a poem—passed around to students, family and friends, no need for even my name on it. Its message was simple: *Keep heart, you are not alone; love, stronger than strong walls, will come, helping your heart in hiding grow wings, feeble perhaps at first, but wings!* Word astoundingly began to come back in 1969, and has continued since, that "Please Hear What I'm Not Saying" was indeed reaching other shores, across space and time was indeed making a difference in other lives.

What follows attests to the power of words from the heart to touch other hearts, sometimes even to change other lives. Read on. You, too, will sing of it.

Chapter 1:
Context and Aftermath

I am sometimes asked what inspired me to write "Please Hear What I'm Not Saying," what my frame of mind was at the time that I wrote it. This is what I can remember.

First some background. I had entered the Society of Jesus (Jesuits) in 1959 after graduating from St. Xavier High School in Cincinnati. Seven years into my training for the priesthood (I left the seminary after my tenth year) I was beginning a three-year stint as an English and Humanities teacher at St. Ignatius College Prep on the near south side of Chicago. It was autumn of 1966 and I had just turned 25.

While appreciating poetry back in high school, I had never given a thought to writing it until encountering a young priest in my early Jesuit years whose enthusiasm for the poetry of Gerard Manley Hopkins and Charles Peguy ignited my soul. I was awakened not only to the beauty and power of the words of Hopkins and Peguy, transmitted by one alive to them, but as a consequence to an exhilarating sudden desire to put down on paper my own words! My fledging efforts perhaps not surprisingly resembled at times Hopkins' compactness and intensity and Peguy's fluid type of free verse, particularly evident, I now recognize, in "Please Hear What I'm Not Saying."

When I sat down to write Please Hear, I did not have it in mind to write a poem. I was simply jotting down ideas that were coming to me, only realizing at the end that, hey, this is kind of a long poem that I could type up and share with some friends and students. Which I did. I had no inkling it would go beyond the people I was giving it to, who knew it was mine, so I didn't even put my name on it. In retrospect I have wondered if my vulnerability in the poem had something to do with leaving off my name.

I had no one in mind that I was writing to but realized by the end, as I put it in the final four lines, that it was really *everyone* I was writing to, because it was everyone, deep down, that I was writing about. I don't recall being either agitated or depressed at the time. I simply was pondering on paper what I had come to believe was a basic human reality—vulnerable, to be sure, but is that not where we all begin our fraught-with-peril-and-promise human journey, and where we remain behind masks and walls until love progressively has given our hearts wings?

What surprised me in the writing of Please Hear was how quickly the poem flowed from me, in but two days as I recall, contrary to my normal grunt and grind efforts with far shorter poems. In retrospect I'm guessing it was precisely because my ego wasn't straining to craft a poem that something long percolating was able spontaneously to rise. I didn't give it further thought until, beginning in 1969, word started getting back to me of publications across the country printing it, conferences using it, people sharing it, and two albums recording it.

I was intrigued to read, for instance, that one of the conferences at the 1973 Association of Humanistic Psychology convention in Chicago was entitled "Please Hear What I'm Not Saying" and decided to attend it. I had no sooner sat down than the conference was begun with a reading of my poem. Imagine my amazement listening to it and then to the spontaneous applause for this poem from an unknown author by an audience of over a thousand people. Then imagine the presenter's amazement afterwards to learn that he was looking at that no longer unknown author. And then there was the woman in one of my counseling groups at Loyola University who was moved to share with us on our final night a favorite poem that she carried everywhere with her. She proceeded to take Please Hear out of her purse and read it to us as her gift to the group.

One of the albums containing Please Hear that an ex-student brought back from college, entitled "Rosko Speaks," remained a mystery to me until I was hitchhiking up the Spanish coast in 1972 and learned from an Englishman giving me a ride that Rosko was a London DJ who recorded albums of his favorite poems. How thrilling to learn that my poem had crossed the ocean!

In all of these early instances of its spreading, the poem's author was "anonymous" or "unknown" or "traditional." You can imagine the incredulity bordering on awe that I felt to realize how far Please Hear was reaching and knowing that the anonymous author was me. It was dawning on me that I had given birth (actually it's more like serving as midwife) to something so deep and true that others, upon discovering it, had to pass it along. The fact that I was personally not getting credit for it seemed unimportant—in fact, I've often mused that its very anonymity may have contributed to its success.

Upon discovering in 1975 another's claim to have written Please Hear (sadly, this was but the first time), I decided that when the time came to publish a collection of my poems I would not only include Please Hear but this time attach my name. The copyrighted volume of poetry that contains "Please Hear What I'm Not Saying," *For the Mystically Inclined,* was published by AuthorHouse (Bloomington, IN) in 2002.

With the internet revolution, the spread of my poem not only across the country but around the world, especially in the past decade, has been little short of phenomenal. The amazing journey of a poem about vulnerability and hope, about how hearts grow wings, clearly is not over yet.

Chapter 2:
The Poem

Please Hear What I'm Not Saying

Don't be fooled by me.
Don't be fooled by the face I wear
for I wear a mask, a thousand masks,
masks that I'm afraid to take off,
and none of them is me.

Pretending is an art that's second nature with me,
but don't be fooled,
for God's sake don't be fooled.
I give you the impression that I'm secure,
that all is sunny and unruffled with me, within as well
as without,
that confidence is my name and coolness my game,
that the water's calm and I'm in command
and that I need no one,
but don't believe me.
My surface may seem smooth but my surface is my mask,
ever-varying and ever-concealing.
Beneath lies no complacence.
Beneath lies confusion, and fear, and aloneness.
But I hide this. I don't want anybody to know it.
I panic at the thought of my weakness exposed.
That's why I frantically create a mask to hide behind,

a nonchalant sophisticated facade,
to help me pretend,
to shield me from the glance that knows.

But such a glance is precisely my salvation, my only hope,
and I know it.
That is, if it's followed by acceptance,
if it's followed by love.
It's the only thing that can liberate me from myself,
from my own self-built prison walls,
from the barriers I so painstakingly erect.
It's the only thing that will assure me
of what I can't assure myself,
that I'm really worth something.
But I don't tell you this. I don't dare to, I'm afraid to.
I'm afraid your glance will not be followed by acceptance,
will not be followed by love.
I'm afraid you'll think less of me,
that you'll laugh, and your laugh would kill me.
I'm afraid that deep-down I'm nothing
and that you will see this and reject me.

So I play my game, my desperate pretending game,
with a facade of assurance without
and a trembling child within.
So begins the glittering but empty parade of masks,
and my life becomes a front.
I idly chatter to you in the suave tones of surface talk.
I tell you everything that's really nothing
and nothing of what's everything,
of what's crying within me.
So when I'm going through my routine
do not be fooled by what I'm saying.
Please listen carefully and try to hear what I'm not saying,
what I'd like to be able to say,
what for survival I need to say,
but what I can't say.

I don't like hiding.
I don't like playing superficial phony games.
I want to stop playing them.
I want to be genuine and spontaneous and me
but you've got to help me.
You've got to hold out your hand
even when that's the last thing I seem to want.
Only you can wipe away from my eyes
the blank stare of the breathing dead.
Only you can call me into aliveness.
Each time you're kind, and gentle, and encouraging,
each time you try to understand because you really care,
my heart begins to grow wings—
very small wings,
very feeble wings,
but wings!

With your power to touch me into feeling
you can breathe life into me.
I want you to know that.
I want you to know how important you are to me,
how you can be a creator—an honest-to-God creator—
of the person that is me
if you choose to.
You alone can break down the wall behind which I tremble,
you alone can remove my mask,
you alone can release me from my shadow-world of panic,
from my lonely prison,
if you choose to.
Please choose to.

Do not pass me by.
It will not be easy for you.
A long conviction of worthlessness builds strong walls.
The nearer you approach to me
the blinder I may strike back.

It's irrational, but despite what the books say about man
often I am irrational.
I fight against the very thing I cry out for.
But I am told that love is stronger than strong walls
and in this lies my hope.
Please try to beat down those walls
with firm hands but with gentle hands
for a child is very sensitive.

Who am I, you may wonder?
I am someone you know very well.
For I am every man you meet
and I am every woman you meet.

September 1966

Chapter 3:
Where First Encountered

The author's website (www.poetrybycharlescfinn.com) invites people to tell where they first heard about "Please Hear What I'm Not Saying." The following sampling of responses indicates the wide spectrum of settings and situations in which the poem was first experienced.

Narcotics Anonymous
Psychology text
English class
Writing workshop
Balcony People by Joyce L. Heatherley
AA sponsor
High school teacher
Grief and loss training
Healing the Child Within by Charles Whitfield
Treatment program for manipulators
Religious education class
Red Cross camp
Communications textbook
Adolescent treatment center
Stephen Covey's book *Seven Habits of Highly Effective People*
Counseling psychology class
AA club
Psych hospital

Alcohol rehab
Walk to Emmaus retreat
College counseling skills class
Drug prevention program
Transactional Analysis class
Dialectical Behavior Therapy group
Chaplain in Marines
Parish youth encounter session
Breaking the Rules by Kurt Wright
Leadership training
Fresh Start for Homeless Women
Retreat discussion group
Army chaplain
Anger management class
4th step AA seminar
Chicken Soup for the Teenage Soul
Psych class in high school
7 Laws of the Learner by Bruce Wilensen
PTSD trauma site
Forum on Suicide
Self-injury site
Youth prayer meeting
Psych hospital critical care
Depression support group
Forensics class
EFT Forum group
Church youth camp
OCPD support group
Bereaved by Suicide group
The Chicken Conspiracy
The Theatre Book of Monologues
Leo Buscalia on PBS
Life Death Transition Workshop (Kubler-Ross)
Young Life
Codependents Anonymous
Marriage Encounter

Air Force school for alcohol and drug counselors
Consulting pairs training at Duke
Posted on a website dedicated to the memory of actor Pete Duhl
Cursillo
Group treatment for rape victims
Spiritual Aspects of Cancer Center
Interprofessional Collaboration Conference
Divorce recovery weekend
Life Issues radio
Youth ministry book
Navy substance abuse program
Winds of Change
Stop When You See Red by Carol Welsh
Pathways
The inspiration for "Welcome to the Masquerade" (1000 Foot Crutch)
I was looking for a piece to perform and wanted something to say "hey this is my life."
Happening weekend retreat
Forum on borderline patients
Book by Fr. John Powell
From a friend who later committed suicide
Imposter Syndrome on Internet
OCPD support website
From the girl I love
Parents of Teens workshop in Michigan
Natural Helpers Training

Chapter 4:
Across America

I just wanted to tell you personally that I came across your poem and I'm speechless. I have been writing for so many years and have read so many poems, and none of them have ever touched me the way your poem did. The words were so deep and with true meaning and I'm sure people who read it can relate on every level. The way you chose your words and how you wrote them—it was seriously breathtaking! I sat up from my desk and just said "wow." I immediately copied it and sent it to everyone I know online. It's one of those poems you have to share with others because you have had such an impact and relation to it, you're positive others will too. I guess what I'm trying to say is that not only is your writing phenomenal but it's a poem I can personally relate to (I too wear my "masks," but I hide it well)...Your wife mentioned on the website that for whatever reason the last two lines are sometimes omitted—THAT IS THE BEST PART! To read your poem and feel the words and experiences, and then to read the ending—that's the part that takes your breath away. It shows unisex feelings that obviously affect us all, some more than others. It shows the readers that it is human to feel the pain and struggle of life and how we all look for acceptance and love...

Hilary, Rhode Island

What a beautifully written, well spoken poem which unveils the heart in each of us. What a difference each of us can make within the lives of those we meet when we approach them from this perspective.

Jodi, Illinois

Thank you for sharing and for putting into words what so many feel, including myself, but don't know how to say it. This is by far THE MOST powerful thing I have read in years and I find it so helpful on my way to recovering from panic, anxiety, agoraphobia, depression and addiction to prescribed opiates. I have tried to hide so many things and found that it is impossible and that I was losing my mind trying to hide. Now I know that hiding behind a mask is too difficult to do for as many years as I have. My mask is slowly coming down so that the real vibrant woman that I truly am can finally be seen in brief glimpses, but I am coming back.

Cindy, South Carolina

I was brought to tears for the first time in many, many years. These words are words which my heart has been crying to write, to say, to have heard, but I have been unable to express it. I have a feeling of hope, of companionship, that others feel this way as well. It is as if these words were taken directly from my being, that someone was able to look into my soul, my fears, my inner most secrets and expose them for what they really are. I thank you, this will be a day in my life that will not be soon forgotten, for a new hope has arisen.

Amanda, New York

This poem has been a mantra for me for surviving, living, and rejoicing. Too often I have put on the brave face while yearning, silently pleading, for someone to see the pain I was in and just talk to me. I am a very proud woman...but sometimes it's to my own detriment...I am absolutely always a survivor and I always told my kids we were a team and were all team players so had to help each other along. I am most proud my kids are best friends and I know that when I die, though they may have spouses and children, they will always have each other...and family means everything. A child, an adult should not go through life craving love but too afraid to admit they need help, guidance, or just plain acceptance....that's why I love this poem so much....it said what was in my heart but too afraid to say out loud should someone laugh or ignore my feelings, as had been done the times I have opened up.

Sandy, Massachusetts

When I was 7 I found this poem and kept it near by all through my childhood. I grew up a foster child, alone and scared. Never knowing what life would toss my way next. I am now 26 and this poem still reaches out to me and in a way makes me feel whole...it gave me hope knowing that somewhere in the world someone cared...I want to say THANK YOU! for giving a lonely child that hope! I now have three children of my own and they will know of this story.

Shel

The first time I heard this poem, I was sitting in a Walk to Emmaus retreat in Asheville, North Carolina, in October. It was in the late 90's... At that time, it sometimes felt like I was barely holding on to life. I found myself wondering why I always ended up in the same place, feeling worthless, uncared for and worn down. It was a mystery to me. A speaker, a woman who had excelled scholastically (she was a Judge before the age of 35) read this poem written in 1966 by Charles C. Finn to about 50 women. As she spoke, my focus centered completely on her, and I was hanging on every word, riveted to my chair. She wasn't just speaking to me, she was exposing me! I know my mouth must have been hanging wide open in shock that I was laid out so vulnerable in front of everyone. When she finished her talk about 45 minutes later, I could hardly move, but I was finally aware that she didn't blow MY cover. I love this poem. It shows that we aren't so different from one another and that the simplest kindness shown to another person can chip away at paralyzing fear and shame so that we can bloom into what God intended us to be.

Natasha, Maryland

So true! The very first time I heard it I wondered who was able to see me, hear me and know me without my disguise. I have a deep love for this poem and have shared it for years since I heard it. You need to know that these words reach deep into so many of us.

John, Kansas

After my dad died in 1980, I was helping my mother clean out his closet which included a bureau with many things that had ridden around in my dad's pockets at one time or another. Keys from hotels from various business trips. Cigar rings. Business cards. And a folded up photo copy of Please Here What I Am Not Saying, as it was titled on the top of the sheet. Somewhere I still have that rumpled version…The fact that my father—a world-renowned neurosurgeon with 8 children—carried this poem in his pocket tells me something important about him. I have always treasured this window into his person, especially since he died when I was still so young (14). I recently discovered this website because I am hoping to include this poem in the readings at my upcoming marriage. I think it is so important that we all understand the frailties and fears of one another, which can help to expand our empathy, understanding, and appreciation of one another.

Rigby, Washington

I found your poem in a book by Brice Wilsensen. He has attributed it to that most prolific of writers "Anonymous"…It has touched me deeply and at age 62 it is exactly what I need to tell a new found love. Thank you for giving me words and courage to express what is in my heart of hearts. Since I am typing this on a computer you won't see the tear-splotched ink, but know that you have once again made the world a little bit safer for the heart.

Richard, Virginia

In 1987 I was challenged by a blessed friend to read this poem she had and to see if I could in any way identify myself in it. Invariably I did and the course it followed was to change my life entirely. I wish there was room here to "tell my story," but suffice it to say, many new roads in life had to be repaved and many had to be redirected as they were headed in the wrong direction. My gratitude for my friend exposing me to this poem and my thankfulness for the writer's inspiration and dedication to creating this work is for me Divine Providence for which my life was to be eternally changed and redirected.

Brian, Wisconsin

I just wanted to say, and it is obvious many people feel this way, but this poem gave me chills, tears, and a sense of happiness all at once. I was crying because it was all true about me and I was happy because I was not the only one out there who felt as such. I love this poem.

Christine, Illinois

This poem speaks for me! All my life I knew there was something different, not right, with me despite appearing quite intelligent and as if I had it all together. Ah, those masks...I did finally discover what my "difference" is; I was diagnosed with severe bipolar, anxiety, and dissociative disorder more than a decade ago (on the verge of turning 40) after undergoing 28-days of treatment for what they thought was chronic depression. A year later I was diagnosed with a thankfully benign but inoperable brain tumor. With these brain issues, I was very much hidden from the world for fear my many illnesses would send people packing...and a few "friends" did go packing. My sister-in-law gave me a copy of "Masks" in 2008 (40 years later this poem's power still speaks loud and clear). It remains a personal favorite and continues to speak directly to my heart. It's as if Mr. Finn looked inside my head and heart and spoke for me of my fears and how I did hide behind so many masks - which therapy has helped to dissolve.

Tamela, Arizona

A friend and counselor mentioned a book I should read called "Healing the Child Within." The book is amazing and helped me recognize and acknowledge some difficult truths. Your poem really spoke to me. It made me realize I'm not alone in this journey. It truly is a poem for all of us.

Steve, Oklahoma

The summer after I graduated from University of Minnesota, a good friend and fraternity brother was killed in a car accident on 8/10/88. Among his things he had in the car was an abbreviated version of this poem, called The Mask. It was cited unknown. It started from the spot "Only you can call me into aliveness." As we went through his things looking for meaning, I remember the chill of this poem...like he was talking to us, begging us to have him live through us. I remember going back to the old fraternity house and typing on one of the only computers on campus, the very first Macintosh. We assembled a program for the funeral service and had an extra page...it soon was filled by The Mask. Every now and again, I think of Paul and I remember what I thought was "The Mask." Tomorrow, I teach Sunday school to college students... Sharing how God helped me through tough times in my young adult stage, I pulled out the now 22 year old funeral program. I wanted to share an old feeling and for some reason was drawn to the internet. Surely someone must have written this poem. Three clicks later, I found "someone." Your gift has served me well for 22 years. I read it today. I wept. I missed Paul. I missed who he might have been. I remembered who he was and the day we thought he talked to us from death...the day he asked us to call him into aliveness. My nine year old came into my office. H saw my tears and he turned away and froze. He did not know what to do. I wept, then asked him to hold me. I explained I missed an old friend. I shared the poem. And as he grows older, I will introduce him to the first half that he missed out on. Perhaps it will serve him as well.

Tom, Missouri

I read this poem to my boyfriend at the time. He looked at me as though I was crazy! I knew then it wouldn't last. This poem is universal. Every honest soul seeker will find something that resonates with them inside this poem.

Tamara, Florida

Thank you for following the leadings of your heart and jotting down a few lines that are transcending time and still touching lives today. I wear fewer masks today because of your poem.

Kate, Maine

Before preaching one Sunday morning, I read *Don't be Fooled by Me* to my congregation. That was probably in the late 1980's. As we drove home, I asked my wife some questions about it. She asked who wrote it. At that time I had to tell her "Anonymous," why? She said it sounded like something I would write. What a compliment! I pastored Baptist churches for 48 years. I also instructed Dale Carnegie courses for 15 years. For many of those years I referenced your poem many, many times. It is fabulous. It describes me and everyone I know! It also makes relating to others quite different. Knowing they are as I am makes relating to them much easier.

Jack, Arkansas

I was shown a copy of your poem in 1986. I painstakingly wrote the whole thing down on a piece of paper in purple ink. I still have it. I have carried it with me everyday since it was shown to me. I have read it over and over until the paper is as soft as silk and the ink has bled from my numerous tears…It was me you had written about. It was my life, my story…You may not fully realize how powerful your words have been to me, but I am here, and if it weren't for your poem, I may not have been. [from her original email]….I am humbled over the fact that you responded to my email. It is obvious that this is not an automatic response. I am not sure how to say thank you, but I am in tears. As I read the original letter to my husband, he listens impatiently. He asks why I am crying. I begin to read your response. His face softened, something that doesn't happen to the rock in our family. Thank you for making our Valentine's Day one of the most powerful we have ever experienced. He understands the impact of your poem…He knows how powerful your poem is to me because I read it to him on our first serious date.

Mindi, West Virginia

This is an incredible message. It is my story. Thank you for allowing God to use your heart.

Leon, Florida

I feel like a bird with a broken wing so you can imagine how this part speaks to me now: "Each time you're kind, and gentle, and encouraging,/ each time you try to understand because you really care,/my heart begins to grow wings--/very small wings,/very feeble wings,/but wings!"... Thank you for a beautiful expression from deep within the heart of all. It's not only a reminder of the pain we all feel but also how we can help each other heal.

Butterfly

This is my favorite poem of all time. It has a place of honor on the back of my door, where only the most important things in my life are placed.

Emily, Georgia

I was reading the book "Healing the Child Within" by Charles Whitfield and I came across this poem. As I began to read it I just started crying realizing that it describes me perfectly. I showed it to my therapist and she was amazed by the poem, she did not realize that I thought this way all the time. I showed it to another friend in my recovery group and she thought I had written it. I said no but it's me and she said it describes her too.

Lori, Nebraska

I have been struggling and heartbroken for 3 years by a failed close personal relationship. The poem strikes home for me not so much as it applies to myself but to the other person. I am very open with my own feelings and thoughts. (In fact my counselor advises me that I need to learn to filter more of what I say and show.....) The other person in this failed relationship always wears a mask, and finds it nearly impossible to be open, honest, and straightforward with their thoughts and feelings. For 3 years, we've been in a strange dance of showing and hiding feelings, misinterpreting the message, and hurting each other. I find the poem extremely helpful in letting go of my anger when this person hurts me by going silent and shutting down. The poem encourages me to step back, be patient, and continue to love, gently. I want to share a quote from George Elliott (Mary Ann Evans) that, for me, illustrates the flip side of this coin: "Oh, the comfort, the inexpressible comfort of feeling safe with a person; having neither to weigh thoughts nor measure words, but to pour them all out, just as they are, chaff and grain together, knowing that a faithful hand will take and sift them, keep what is worth keeping, and then, with a breath of kindness, blow the rest away."

Jeff, North Carolina

I have never read anything that summed me up so perfectly. I was raised by hurtful and uncaring parents that have scarred me physically and emotionally. Now that I am a father it scares the hell out of me that the wounds from my past will affect my beautiful child so I am doing everything I can to make sure this does not happen. One of those things is reading a book titled, "Healing the child within: discovery and recovery for adult children of dysfunctional families," and that is where I came upon your amazing poem.

Scott, Michigan

I still have a yellowed with age copy of "Don't Be Fooled By Me" with no author shown. It was given to a retreat discussion group by a Catholic Brother who could not tell us who the author was but it fit in well with the group since some of the men were having problems with troubled teens. Ironically, at the same retreat house, I can't remember if it was the same year or a later retreat, there was a Redemptorist Priest there who was a sculptor, and he had sculptured a statue of a man removing a facial mask to reveal his true self.

Henry, Maryland

Thank you for this poem! After reading some of the comments on this site from other individuals that have been touched by this poem, I realize I wasn't the only one that felt like this. I was doing some cleaning and came across it with old letters from friends and ex-girlfriends. I too started to write it long hand as I wanted to express what I couldn't say to a girlfriend. I have been in and out of foster homes since I was 8 yrs old. Now at 33, I've tried to figure out why I've pushed people away all my life. Growing up the way I did, you try to get comfortable with the new families. I would start to get attached thinking I would have a new family and as soon as that would happen, I would get shipped off to another home to start over. I learned to put that wall up very early, always scared of losing people you start to care about. This affected my relationships and most recently my marriage. It's been a long road and I have pushed people that I have loved away and it hurt, but I was safe because I knew that I could rebound, stay behind that wall, and wear my masks to hide how I felt. I now know that I don't have to do that anymore and this poem reminds me of that. Thanks again for saying what I couldn't say.

Jody, Washington

This poem was given to me many years ago from a friend. When I first got it, I didn't really read it. Even after that, I didn't get its full meaning. Today I can read it and it can bring me to tears.

Juggs, Tennessee

This is the most BEAUTIFUL self describing writing I have ever had the fortune to read...It is so very to the point, and true...it's heart-stopping...What a wonderful revelation it brought about for me. Thank you for the validation of self.

Michelle, Nevada

Your poem is timeless. It is a view into the heart of man.

David, Rhode Island

I was saved by what someone once told me was "A God's Deal" and with her help and that hand that she held out and I took hold. She gave me that poem and it's gotten me though difficult times in life. I don't know where she is anymore, but the poem hangs on my wall and I look at it when times get hard. And I hear her voice and the words that saved my life. SHE HEARD WHAT I WAS NOT SAYING.

Velvet, Texas

Thank you for midwifing these very important words and for listening to the Divine Spark within YOU!!! I cannot read it without crying especially if I am sharing/reading it to another. It was given to trainees and participants of the 1991 "Life, Death and Transition" Workshop of Elizabeth Kubler-Ross. I have shared it with many people as an unknown author poem.

Pat, Vermont

See how God is using your special poem. Thank you for touching my heart and my life and also my family's life.

Cathy, Oklahoma

I remember hearing this poem late at night on WNEW FM, New York, in 1970. It touched me that it was really me the poem was about. They read it, I believe it was a DJ named Rosko or something like that, I scrambled feverishly to write parts of it down every time I heard it. I've kept a copy in my papers ever since. I lost track of how many people I gave it to, Sorry, I thought there was no name attached to it, author unknown. We were discussing it with our son and I was looking for it when I thought of using the internet. Upon finding the poem and this site I thought I would write a short note to say thank you. There was only one addition to the poem I had heard, after " For I am every man you meet, I am every woman you meet." Someone added I AM YOU.

Dave, New Jersey

The LP album, given to me by a former student returning from college in 1970, was entitled Rosko Speaks. *There indeed was no name other than "Traditional" attached to the poem which was entitled "I am You." Who Rosko was remained a mystery to me until, hitchhiking up the Spanish coast in 1972, I learned from an Englishman giving me a ride that Rosko was a London DJ with albums of poetry out (his own and others). How thrilling to realize Please Hear had made it across the ocean!*

Someone gave it to me from a book I can't recall. I couldn't keep the book so I hand wrote it and kept it in my wallet for years, sharing it with people that I thought could use its wisdom. I still get teary-eyed thinking of them as they read it. About 2 hours ago I was going through some books in my closet and found the very paper I had handwritten so long ago and decided to google it and found this page. Thank You Mr. Finn for the opportunity to share this with so many who were greatly influenced by your words. I shall keep the tradition that I have with your poem alive till my last breath (hopefully a long time in the future) and hope others with do the same.

WG, Texas

Someone (I still don't recall who) gave this to me when I was going through a miserable (is there any other kind???) divorce from a man who had a bad habit of chasing other women while still married to me. As I read it, I remember the words getting pretty blurry because I was crying so hard. After some time, I put it away somewhere and it was "lost" for 25 years. The other night, I was looking on the internet for employment as I lost my job 8 months ago. I was feeling pretty rejected by the world (not easy to find employment in this economy), and for some reason, this poem flashed into my head. I hadn't thought about it for years and couldn't remember the exact title, but somehow, through the cobwebs, it finally crystallized and I entered it into GOOGLE. Up it came. I was thrilled. As expected, the words got all blurry again (tears) and after a little reflection, I sent it out to 7 of my closest friends. I know you've touched millions of lives with this. It just touched mine (again)....and 7 others.

Toni, Minnesota

I have loved your poem for over two decades and have shared it ever since it was introduced to me at a critical point in my own healing journey.

Gail, Connecticut

Deeply lonely as a child this hit me at the perfect time at 18...from being a stripper to blossoming into an engineer this poem has haunted and healed me. I find your clarity of introspection amazing in this literary masterpiece. I cannot thank you enough. Somehow I feel less alone.

Regina, Nevada

While in the US Army at the Presidio during 1973-77 it was 'passed around' to a group of counselors at the Alcohol and Drug Abuse Prevention and Control Program (Whew!). I next saw it in about 1996 as the work of a 14 year old student at Mitchell High School in Colorado Springs, CO (My daughter said the student got class credit for it as her own creation!). This morning it suddenly surfaced in my thoughts as 'Don't Be Fooled By Me.' I Googled it (Happy Day!) and was rewarded by what I believe to be the original copy by C. C. Finn. At age 80 it has been an inspiration to me for over 30 years.

Bill, New York

I had recently gone through a divorce and was very depressed so my Army Chaplain suggested that I attend this personal growth retreat sponsored by the Navy Chaplains Society. It was there that I first experienced the power of this poem.

Derek, Florida

I am a freshman at Bowling Green State University...I was first introduced to Please Hear What I'm Not Saying at Natural Helping training in 1988. They gave us an adapted version of your poem called Masks. I immediately fell in love with it. When I looked up the full version, I was even more moved. As a poet myself, I really feel the need to commend you. Your poem captures what I, as a poet, have always tried to do, the complexity of human emotion. You gave us all an insight into ourselves.

Brian, Ohio

A small group leader recited the poem as a monolog during the weekend. I did not realize until several weeks later that she was reciting a poem. I have a copy in my college scrapbook that I re-typed. The version is only slightly different from the original. I illustrated the poem with photos for my final project for my Photography 101 project in 1985.

Dede, Florida

I heard a small part of this poem from a friend of mine, years ago. I was so instantly enamored by it I looked it up online, only to discover it was much longer than I realized. It is easily one of the best poems I have ever read. I often like to read this poem when I'm feeling upset, because it always makes me feel better afterword. It lets me know I'm not alone.

Danielle

To me it's a passionate love song about my life and who I am. NO ONE understands me like the poem does. I'm now 50 yrs. old. My inner child is still crying. No one is listening. Still.

Cathy, Vermont

This poem was read to a class of displaced home makers at the Hannah Harrison Career School in Washington, DC in 1981. The teacher found it in the book Masks. She had us close our eyes as she read it and gave out copies. I kept it all these years, giving out copies to different people. It changed my perspective on the fear within me. I was not alone.

Edris, Washington, DC

I have been diagnosed and currently going through psychotherapy for DID [Dissociative Identity Disorder] and this poem is a replica of who we are. The mask we wear for assurance, acceptance, love, and all the things any person desires that wasn't there when growing up. Its going to be a long and bumpy road for my girl and my ex along with my son as we begin to develop into who we are with just one personality, not many as we do now.

Jeff, Ohio

I can honestly say that this poem saved my life, even in the abbreviated state that I got it in. I was heading in the wrong direction, fast, a path of self destruction. But it made me realize how high and how strong I had built walls that I wasn't going to let anyone through. It changed me. From there I got the help that I needed and slowly started to let those around me that loved me break down those walls. I actually owe you my life, and God of course for letting this poem fall into my hands.

Patricia, Michigan

I remember reading and passing on your poem to others back in the 1970's while working in the Navy substance abuse program...I believe that everyone that has read your poem has made the statement "this is me"...I believe that what you call a reflection is a "Spiritual revelation" to share with others...I think that your poem illustrates very well how we are manipulated into bearing false witness against ourselves by putting on the many faces that we wear to hide our inner essence from others.

Randy, Oregon

This poem touched me some 20 years ago. At that time it was listed as "Author Unknown." However, as the years have passed, this poem has never been far from my mind, especially during troublesome times. I am someone with bipolar disorder, and when I was trying to understand how I felt and get others to reach out, this poem was an invaluable tool - a gift - words that I could not speak myself, but felt.

No name given

I cried when I found this among my father's papers following his death in 2003. My father was a tough guy, and one who grew up hiding his soft side. My father physically abused me until I was sixteen years old, and verbally abused me my entire life. While I would go through many periods of not talking to him, I never gave up on him, for I was one who could see his mask. I tried desperately to reach out my hand and love to him, and was always hurt for my efforts. I never, ever gained the acceptance of my father, and for this I am still suffering as a 48- year old woman. I know that my father loved me, and he, in turn, had been abused by his father, and was only doing what he thought "fathers

25

were supposed to do." I could see his pain, and tried to reach him on a deeper level, but I was always ridiculed. My own "mask," you see, was being tough enough to take the abuse from him, when really, inside, I was just a scared little girl who wanted my daddy to love me. For the rest of my single, celibate days on this earth I will want this, and I will never get those words I desperately need from him, now that he is gone. My entire family is like this, and I have seen it to be my "job" to try to change myself and to reach out the loving hand that they all need. I am constantly attacked for this, since the act of doing this brings light to the very mask itself, and people don't want to admit it. I don't mean to reveal anyone's weakness; I just want to show them the love that I know could heal them. Still today, my family hurts me. Right now, I am a recluse because so many people have pushed my hand and love away. I spend most of my days alone, afraid of being hurt ... again. Ironically, whenever and wherever I go, when I do go anywhere, I am filled with love for all, help people wherever I can, and have a smile and a kind word for everyone. The world opens up, and I can see a path spreading far and wide as my love for all envelopes all those I come into contact with. However, eventually, I run into someone who knocks me off this loving path, just like my father used to do with his fists and his words, and I fall into a lonely existence once more. I hope my story serves to remind people not to push that hand away, when it comes to you filled with love and acceptance, and NOT to take it personally as a sign that you are weak. It is the greatest strength to take that mask off, to change into a better person, a person who truly, sincerely LOVES and ACCEPTS other humans. Can you imagine if everyone just gave in to this, and realized that in doing so, the world would be transformed?

Donna, California

I thoroughly enjoyed your poem. I must have read it at least 50 times and it just inspires me. It gives me a sensation that I have not felt in a while, a feeling of not being totally alone. I can only wish that some day someone who is kind and strong will with good intentions break down my wall. Until that day, I will remember your poem and try to hear what others are not saying.

Athia

This poem touched my very soul.

Randy, Texas

This poem has touched so many people that just I know. It is amazing.

Jeff, Tennessee

The poem and others came up when I did a Stumble Upon search that responded to one of my interests listed with them; poetry. My eyes rounded and I read it 3 times. I used to feel exactly like that - guess I always will to some degree, even now as I reach 70.

Susan, Florida

We've been listening to the Steven Covey tape while we drive. When he read your poem, we were riveted to the words. Marvelous! Makes you think, and think deeper.

Linda, California

This poem is a "slam dunk" description of me. I have struggled with "Imposter Syndrome" forever. All of my accomplishments in my life have been "excused" away in my own mind by telling myself I was "lucky" and if anyone REALLY discovered how dumb I am, I'd be in real trouble. I'd lose my job and wouldn't be able to support my daughter, and my mother would be right in the end...she would always tell me, "you'll never make it". And my high school counselor would be right about the path I picked for going to college..."it's tough, I don't know if you can do it." I have a B.S. in Computer Science from a respected University, but even when I got the piece of paper, I thought to myself..."well, if so-and-so wouldn't have helped me in whatever class, I'd never have this diploma." It's been a crazy struggle to accept within myself that I'm okay, I have accomplished some things and I'm really competent in my job, and people LIKE me and RESPECT me because I make their jobs easier. I'm still struggling with it and I'm 47 years old. This poem hits home because I have always felt like I'm a facade, everything seems to work out okay (somehow!), I always get by and no one "finds out" how incompetent I really am. But I should prepare for when they do find out. God, it's been an endless feeling of being trapped in my own mind. When my son died, I didn't have the same feelings of hiding anything. I grieved alone because I'm an introvert, but I never had the same feelings that someone would "find out" what really happened. That situation seemed more cut and dried. It's the feeling of living and working where I think someone will "find me out," that I'm really not what they think I am. In closing, again, this poem has hit home with me and gives me another step in realizing that maybe I really am being self-destructive. It does seem that I'm wearing a mask every day of my life and the words, "don't be fooled by me, don't be fooled by the face I wear" shout from inside me with almost every person I meet. Thanks for taking the time to read this. I'm still on a long road to being comfortable with myself, and thanks for letting me share.

Karen, Nebraska

I found this after the birth of my premature son. This related so much to me. I felt that I was presenting a calm surface, but inside there was a storm. I was pretending that things did not bother me. I wanted to hide the mess I felt I was. I did not want people to enter my home. So many times, the glance was not followed by acceptance.

Angie, Washington

When I first read it I felt as though I was reading what my husband can not tell me. I felt the words deep within my spirit. I felt so much compassion and love for him. I didn't want to cry while I was reading it, as I was just about to leave to go somewhere, but I am glad that it touched me like it did. I want so badly to be able to love him enough for him to take off his "mask." We have been married for 16 years and I have struggled trying to get to know him. I have been considering divorce, but after reading this poem, I feel the renewed strength to keep trying to unconditionally love my husband and pray that I can be the one to help him remove his mask and finally let himself feel true love. Thank you for being a strong enough spirit to share what so many people feel and sense in others that they love.

Rosanne, California

Thank you for this beautiful poem, "Please Hear What I'm not Saying," that says so much about the depth of who we really are. I read this poem years ago while attending a local business college and of course the author was "anonymous." It's so nice to finally put a name and a face with your poem. I've just forwarded this poem to a friend and hopefully it will touch them as it touched me years ago. Thank you again for giving us a way to say what we don't know how to say.

Debbie, Ohio

I cannot try to explain the impact your poem has had on me through my life. I found your poem in what I remember to be a local newspaper on Long Island when I was a teen in 1972. For some reason, this poem, and none other that I ever recall, has meant more to me than words can express. I remember wanting to somehow preserve what I had read. I went to my father's desk and made many attempts on a manual typewriter to copy the poem in its entirety. Wanting a nice finished product, and without the benefit of a word processor or a spell checker, each time I mistyped, I started a new sheet. As I transcribed through and reached the end of the poem, for some reason, I remember thinking I would leave off the last two lines, somehow feeling it had more of an impact leaving the reader wondering who this "person" was. I neglected to alter the poem however, and was finally successful in rendering it to an unblemished piece of cotton weave typing paper. I bought a cheap glass frame and hung it in my bedroom. To this day, 32 years later, it has moved with me at least a half dozen times and now has a place of prominence on my office wall.

Steve, Virginia

I have read the INCREDIBLY WARM, HONEST, HEART WRENCHING & FANTASTICALLY INSPIRING LOVE book 'Mister God This Is Anna' several times...wondered if Fynn & Anna are real persons...and this morning just now read Please Hear What I Am Not Saying that came via my pc from www.ChristAsUs.com (friends I know). I am so glad that Fynn is real and you and family have a website.

Alice, Connecticut

I too have cherished this poem for many many years. I first read it in a book titled Balcony People and it said that the author was unknown. It was just today that I was thinking about the poem and wanted to share it with some girlfriends of mine that I decided to google it instead of typing it word for word from the book and I came across your website. How awesome to get the story behind such a lovely piece of work! It speaks to billions, it touches all and it will for ever and ever!

Elva, Ohio

In learning to live again with a spouse, I use your poem to describe my innermost, secret and sacred feelings of who I really am. Thank you for writing this and for touching my life.

Deb, Arkansas

It's funny how this poem never changes but the meaning of it does over time...This poem was given to me a long time ago. When I first really read it I thought, how could anybody feel this way. I was a pretty optimistic person back then. Now I understand more about wearing masks.

Allen, Tennessee

Thanks again for coming up with this wonderful depiction of interior discussion, self evaluation, and turmoil.

John, Minnesota

I still remember the day I found your poem "Please Hear What I Am Not Saying" more than 10 years back through an autobiography of a physically disabled girl named Jane. She has shared this poem in her novel and I was so touched by it that this is the very first poem that I actually copied down.

Jessi

Now it's like I have in words how I feel inside.

David, Pennsylvania

You can see what other people don't take the time to see...It made me appreciate my best friend even more because I thought not even she knew, but I guess she did.

Jennie, New Hampshire

In the entire book "the child within," what connected and moved me the most was your poem. I sob, recognizing myself in it. Every night, before I go to bed, I read your poem to help me accept who I am, to heal my child within. I will share with my dear friends your marvelous piece...Merci.

P

I LOVE THIS POEM!!!!!!!!!!!!THIS IS A GREAT POEM FOR ALL OF US WHO LIVE IN THE WORLD.

Judy, Texas

"Please Hear" is such an amazing and beautiful poem. I cried when I first read it. It is so real and touches so deep. I'm positive that as long as there is literature, this poem will be remembered. It's the stuff of legends.

Jade, Hawaii

Please Hear OPENED A VERY, VERY LARGE DOOR TO HELP A LOT OF PEOPLE SOCIALLY, PSYCHOLOGICALLY, AND SPIRITUALLY...I think I am going to write a book, you gave me the inspiration.

Merv, New York

I am struck by your insight and was deeply moved for the simple fact that you write about how many people feel but don't talk about. You put into words what I have experienced for a good part of my adult life in dealing with depression.

Joni, Minnesota

Be joyful about your poem. You my friend have made such a difference.

Marna, Oregon

I wasn't looking for your poem when it found me today. I'm so glad it did. It touched my heart and brought tears to my eyes before I even realized it. Thank you for not being afraid to share it with the world.

Lee Ann

Thank you for not only having the insight and talent to write the poem, but also for having the courage to share the poem...I have kept it on my cork board and still get goose bumps when I read it.

Diane, North Carolina

I am here to say this poem is priceless. I truly believe this is part of the cure for the 21st century.

Daryl, Colorado

It ripped through my very being and said everything that I was feeling and thinking and still does...It's like you know the whole world and what really goes on in the minds of others. I made it my mission to memorize the entire poem so that even if I lost the only copy I had I would always have it in my heart and mind.

Charlotte

Your poem moved me. I am also a poet, more usually a writer of literary fiction/stories, but the older I get the more I think about poetry as an arrow to the heart, or the heavens. Thank you for sharing your poem— for your arrow to the world.

Susie

Your poem brought us together. We became really good friends after that moment. We help each other out by removing our mask piece by piece, little by little, taking all the time we need. Till this day we are very close friends and I believe we always will just because of your poem. Today all my friends know the real me and not what my mask said I was...I rewrote your poem and I hung it on my wall...

Alyssia, California

I have cherished your poem for decades…Thank you for your light in the world.

Tamara, North Carolina

I can relate to this poem so much…It tells the truth about me that I fear all to know. I thank you for your wisdom. I thank you for my voice when I cannot speak.

Caitrin

This poem changed my life, as did Consulting Pairs Training at Duke University in 1994 where I first heard it.

Suzanne, NC

I carried a paper around in my wallet for a few months to write phone numbers on and one day I was cleaning all the bad skeletons out of it. When I turned it over I read this poem and I could not believe how much this sounded like me and how I feel. Thank you for showing me the true me.

Charles, Ohio

The poem is remarkable and yes it touches and will continue to touch lives throughout time I suppose.

Cynthia, Florida

I read your poem for the first time a couple years ago, not really understanding it. As I found it again recently on the internet and experienced some things myself, I truly begin to understand the meaning of the poem. I think your poem is great and shows the world the silent plea of mankind.

Edwin

After reading this poem I felt as though you reached inside and found all of me.

Char, Maryland

This poem touches a place deep inside all of us and everyone who reads the poem is forever changed in some way.

Jen, Ohio

This poem so describes me. I hid behind masks after masks for fear that people can see the real vulnerable me. The confidence they see is just a shield to protect myself from them.

Carine

Thanks for the inspiring poem. I really enjoyed reading it. I just hope a lot of people will pick up the message as they digest each line and discard lovely or hard facades that conceal so much turmoil and anguish, fears and insecurities. I pray that the message of this poem will heal a lot of wounds and help us all to go out confidently into the world and be a blessing to others.

Roselyne

I am a fourth year RN student and was doing my psychiatric rotation when I first encountered your poem. I was waiting for group to begin and was just aimlessly wandering the hall, reading the miscellaneous inspirational works they have posted along it. I, for the most part, skimmed what was there—but the title alone of your poem caught me. I was struck from the first word to the last. I do not believe there is a single person that this poem would not speak to on some level. It touched me so much that I pulled the writing off the wall and photocopied it.

Siobhan

I do not know who gave your poem to me, but I do know that it was many years ago, typed on an old typewriter...Obviously you have expressed a heart cry of many...I have passed it around all over for the last 15 years—to churches, Bible Study groups, and individuals.

Diane

My father gave it to me over 20 years ago. It always reminds me that there is a heart in all of us. It doesn't make me weak nor taken with rescuing everyone I meet. It empowers me with strength knowing we are all of the same make-up. In return I try to empower others with understanding.

Kathryn

Chapter 5:
Around the World

It is a really beautiful poem. My girlfriend read me this poem when I visited her. It touched my heart. Poem talks the true about us. All of us need love. But the first we must open our heart to each other and then the love is coming.

Mitja, Slovenia

Thank you for this wonderful poem. When I first read it I had to stop several times to wipe away the tears. My therapist gave me this book to read. I grew up in a very dysfunctional family and lived with sexual, emotional and verbal abuse. My past has controlled my life for more than 40 years. I didn't know how to be me. I have hidden for so long and trying to describe myself to others was impossible to put into words. With this poem I now have the words. My first reaction to this poem was "this is me, how could this be?" Every word, every line, every emotion was me. This is how I have lived my life. I am just beginning the healing journey and the road ahead is very long, but I know that I will carry this poem and its message with me until I am no more. Bless you for speaking/writing what some of us had no words to express.

K.B., Ontario, Canada

This poem was shown to me by a friend of mine and the moment I read it I knew I had found the answer to a long standing question inside me

- "Is it just me or is everyone like this?" I was at the time going through this extremely difficult phase of getting to know who I really am, and this poem was like a revelation to me, and to think it was something I always knew, just needed to come out to the surface. It is a reality hidden inside all of us, but playing this masquerade becomes second nature and we don't even realise what we ourselves are up to. All I can say is this poem touched my heart very deeply and I will cherish it all of my life, and later probably when my children will need some sage words of advice I would hand them a copy too.

Sanchari, India

I thank you dear sir for finding the words to express my deepest feelings from within. My Inner Child thanks you for acknowledging her cries for help. I was once trapped inside a cocoon of my own making, but now I am breaking free and embracing who I am and have always been.

Cindy, Australia

Thought you might like to know that I am struggling to memorize this poem. I do poetry at the coffee house, and decided to do yours. The first time that I read this, it was at the funeral of a woman that I had met at Church. She had died recently after an operation. No one knew her very well, she was new in town. No husband, and a grown-up daughter that she wasn't getting along with, maybe 30 years old, and she was about 50ish. So, she died, and people were urged to go along to the funeral (from the church), to fill up the room more or less, since her daughter would be there, and so I put this poem into my pocket and off I went. The minister didn't know the woman very well, and invited anyone that had something to say to speak, so I took your poem and shared it. As always when I have read it, the room was totally still. After the funeral, a number of people came over to tell me how much they had liked it, especially the psychiatric nurses that were there, and that had been working with the woman, as well as many others. So I thank you. I only thought to look for you, as I am struggling to memorize this poem, some 7 or 8 years later!...What I especially like, and what frightens me a bit, is the subtle kindness of attitude that reveals itself, the trust in the poem. I feel encouraged to "hear" more of what I am hearing, and respond to it, since I have been memorizing the poem. It is making a difference in my life!

Sharon, British Columbia, Canada

I came across your poem and it brought me tears. Thank you! As I read it, I thought to myself how amazing that someone has captured in a poem exactly how I am currently feeling. And then when I reached the end I felt relief that it isn't only me or a few, but everyone that feels this way. So I'm not alone. That's my relief. I feel relief and less fear to reach out and take chances with others.

Kelly, France

Today in religion education class our professor included this poem into our regular prayer. I was amazed. Every single word described me perfectly. I googled it as soon as I got home and I now have it written down. It feels great knowing that there are many people who feel the same as well as having all those feelings formed into words in such a beautiful way. I am certain it'll stay with me and I'll keep rereading it.

Maris, Croatia

The copy we found had a title of "Don't Be fooled by me." Wanting to know who wrote it I Googled it and found the original. I love the simplicity of it, and how it has stuck a chord with all who read it. For the words are true for all who read it. I loved it.

John, England

Dealing with depression, I related to the poem quite deeply to the point of being able to identify the masks. Many masks to hide the true feelings deep down, scared of what people would think of a male crying every night before bed..."Please hear what I'm not saying" helped me seek help from others to break the walls of depression, to allow others into my life and to show emotions. Exposing my weakness helped me build my strengths again by building friendships.

Aaron, Australia

It just grabbed me and explained how I am - my masks. A wonderful poem.

Ellen, Scotland

I really love this poem. It gives me a new thought about courage.

Chiaki, Saipan

I read your poem "Every Man and Every Woman." I just had to tell you how it moved me. Totally unprepared for life outside, having been in care from 2 until 15, leaving in 1959. Having been raised without having a voice, without the ability to think for yourself, without the chance to fight your corner, how to decide what to wear and what to eat, how could I possibly cope with the difficulties of mixing with people. These people I might add, that were on the outside, I was raised to believe were superior to me. So why should I want to fight back against bullying and dominating talk. I always felt inferior and why not, when my own parents did not want me, did not fight to have me with them. They just carried on making a life for themselves, making my rejection feel even worse. Thankfully I have woken up to who I am today and although I still find it extremely difficult dealing with people in authority, I can finally fight my corner.

Patricia, UK

This has been a part of my life since my friend read it to me over the telephone 42 years ago. I never knew who wrote it, only that it struck a chord then and still does today! I was estranged from my father for years and I gave the poem to him to read, but alas he didn't "get it." I have shared the poem with many people over the years, and it strikes that same chord in them as it did for me.

Cat, British Columbia, Canada

Wow! What a powerful message you convey in your poem. It's so easy to think that I am the only one who is "misunderstood." Reminds of St. Francis' prayer, "Lord, help me not so much to seek to be loved but to love with all my soul, etc." Thank you for this. I am going through a rather difficult time in my life with somebody very close to me. You have inspired me to look beyond the "mask."

Ursula, South Africa

I came across this poem. It spoke to me about being authentic…I am sure it has been read by thousands, maybe millions, of people around the world. I have often referred to it as a teacher and have explained that this is what I endeavour to follow and encouraged other women and my students to do the same.

Sharon, London, England

I find that the poem lets me see deeply and stay true to the gold below the mask.

Joban, India

I am so pleased to be able to send a message to the person who produced those heart touching words that describe the feeling of being human so very, very well.

Maureen, Manchester, England

A week ago a friend of mine send me a poem by Rudyard Kipling, "If." And just looking for the translation of it, I found yours. Reading "If," I felt like having someone's soul in my hand. Reading yours - I felt like having my own soul on my desk. This was so strange, but so touching experience. The words I would never dare to write, I just forwarded to the friend. And never we had so open conversation like this one, just exchanging poetry. I hope one day I will learn to speak so openly about myself.

Weronika, Poland

I was handed this poem by my therapist several years ago and it's my only way of being able to explain to other people how I feel when there's no way of explaining it.

UK

Our tutor read it out and gave us a copy, it said author unknown. The words are so deep and meaning full and true to me. I could really identify with all of it and so desperately was scared for someone to 'hear me.' Then I did want to be 'heard.' The poem has stuck with me throughout and I have thought about it often while listening to other people & friendships. Now it's time to listen for me & take the hand that's offered.

Alison, England

I'm sure I will be reiterating what has been said many times before but "Please Hear What I Am Not Saying" has touched my life in a very special way... You have given a great gift to me and countless others.

Rod, British Columbia, Canada

This often comes to mind when meeting people in a social setting.

Cheryl, South Africa

When I first read it I was awestruck. I felt it spoke from my heart about me. It speaks to you. I find it a gripping poem. It is so sad. Everyone should read it. There is such hope within it and yet a reality that it may never be.

Michael, Ireland

Over the years I have built this wall of insecurity. It started when I was very young growing up in Winnipeg, Manitoba. Being of German ancestry created problems as I was born in 1938 at the beginning of World War 2. I joined toastmaster about 6 months ago to overcome my fright of public speaking. This has helped me to come out of my shell...I love your poem "Hear What I Am Not Saying" as it digs deep into our soul.

Mel, British Columbia, Canada

I had goosebumps when I had searched and read the original poem and discovered its history. When I was in highschool, my sister shared it to me. I read it and "MY," I thought, "this is me..." I felt very close to the poem that it seems to have been written by me. It was very personal to me that I made it a reflection of myself. I misplaced the copy my sister gave me and just now, I found it again. I read it out loud and tears started to fall. I wanted to read this to everyone I know to let them see the real me.

Sheena, Philippines

Please Hear is a great and wonderful poem I have ever read. Your poem touches the heart and makes me much younger.

Tshering, Bhutan

I read this poem when I was a teenager over 25 years ago. I have always kept this poem as it really reflected a lot of who I felt I was - with the context of all of the masks that I wore; and still wear now. I did not know who wrote this poem, that is until today. I am not sure where I cited the poem, but I have always held onto this poem and recently I read it out to my fellow students in a social sciences class.

Maryann, New Zealand

When I found your poem, I could understand the meaning, but it took me a few times to translate it into spanish in a good language. Really the time I used is not a lost time. Your poem is wonderful. I know that all of us have the same problem with masks, from our birthday we are learned to use it. The big problem comes later, years later when we want to take off the masks, because other people do not want to hear you, and they go away when you really want to show your real self. It is horrible to feel again the reject on you by the others when what you want is only to be yourself. That's something I can not really understand, at the time you are yourself, you still are more alone. Thanks a lot for share your poem with me. Muchas gracias por compartir tu poema conmigo.

Domingo, Spain

I fall in love with a man who has a big fear about showing who he really is. He is wearing several kind of masks and cheats everybody around him. In one hand it makes him happy, because he is able to protect himself and in the other hand he is sad, because no one sees who he really is. I found out about a kind of illness we call schizoide Persönlichkeitsstörung in german. These people who are touched by that are scared about showing feelings, but cry inside of themself, cause they are standing alone and feelings and love is what they are missing. He was very often cold to me, but behind all that is standing a big fear. I've read a lot about that kind of people, with that kind of problem. So I found your poem. It gives me hope and shows me a view of a person who feels like that. Thank you!

Tabea-Sophie, Germany

Tanto a mi hijo como a mi nos impresionó mucho el poema de CHARLES C. FINN, porque recoge nuestra verdadera realidad ante la vida y ante situación específicas que afrontamos en dl día a día. Supe de la existencia de ese hermoso poema por el compartir de una amiga en el estudio del libro A Course in Miracles.

Gustavo, Columbia

Your poem 'Please Hear What I'm Not Saying' is the only poem that sticks out in my mind among serious poems. I had a poetry class in college. I wrote poetry in high school and college. I've read a few poems too. This one is king. There is insight in this poem. Sometimes I tell people that if you view someone through compassion or mercy you will learn about that person. I believe that. Only tonight I learned that you were a professional counselor. I've thought of that career for myself. I think we may be the same kind of people. We care about people...your words have resonated with me. I'm 35, teaching English in Korea for now...I appreciate your famous poem so very much. I don't know how many times I've read it.

Roy, Korea

its great

Ram, Palestine

I am a member of a well respected depression support site and someone posted a link to the poem. I and many others found the poem very powerful and it rang so true.

Eve, Australia

THANK YOU! Your poem is awesome, and I know it touches everyone's heart when they read it.

Carwen, Cornwall, UK

I chanced to hear the poem in 2001 during my work with young people at the "Jugendbildungsstätte Marstall Clemenswerth" (a meeting place for young people which are interested in building their charakter and identity in communication with others, people which want to think about their lives and their possibilities and which want to reflect about the meaning of life...) We used the poem to get into conversation with the people around us. Since that time the poem accompanies me in my thoughts.

Carina, Germany

Your words touched my soul. Thank you for that. I admire every man who is capable of translating his thoughts and magic inside himself into words.

Ana, Croatia

I have been receiving counseling for depression after the suicide of a good friend. This has brought up other issues of loss and abandonment I had as a child. Since I went for this help I realised that I didn't know who I was. The reason? I have been wearing a mask since I was a child for protection. My counsellor gave this to me and again it was by anonymous. I had to find out who had written these words which affected me so powerfully like no other written word has. These words punched through to my core and made me understand something about myself.

Jim, England

I want to thank you for this wonderfull poem which helps me so much in my life.

Kathryn, Switzerland

I first came across this splendid poem when I helped to organise an Anger Management session for employees of the company I work for. The training was done by a well known trainer who asked us all to read this poem out loud. When I read it, it felt like someone had been watching me all my life and had written about ME! Fascinating! You know, even though that poem is 40 years old, it will remain timeless and be read through the ages! And connect people all over the world.

Sasi, Kuala Lumpur, Malaysia

It was in 1998 that I first heard your poem, but I know it reached the Philippines even before that. I'm sure it has touched millions of Filipinos. I was 8 when I first heard it from my sister, who's 6 years older than me. She loved it so much that she spent time to memorize it. I didn't completely understand what it really meant back then but I already know that it is a very beautiful masterpiece. I asked my sister for a copy of it and still have that copy. As I have grown up I've learned to understand and appreciate it more. It helps me a lot in dealing with other people. I've learned to be honest with what I feel and think.

Em, Philippines

Thank you.......an inspiration for every generation and a guide on this lonely road we have come to know as life...Even at 60 it paused me to wonder!!!

Matt, Dubai

The sentiments in this poem apply to every single one of us. If only more of us lived by them and looked behind the masks we all wear, instead of taking what people show as being what they are, the world would be a much better place.

LW, UK

I was severely depressed just before my fortieth birthday and have no clear memory who gave me the copy of your poem. I do remember clearly its impact and how it helped me regain my self esteem and confidence.

Gillian, Scotland

I was given this at a hospital in 1980. Since then I have passed it on many times. Tonight I passed it on to a lady in England I met on the net who is going through some hard times. I know it will help her as it has helped me.

Janet, Nova Scotia, Canada

In my religion course in Germany we heard this poem and it was the first poem everybody was touched by! It is unbelievable what this poem expresses and how 'real' it is. Thank you for giving the world such a great gift.

Ruth, Germany

Thank you for the poem. As you can see it has traveled all the way down under. It's a wonderful poem. It puts grief at a more understandable level.

Jacquie, New Zealand

Just thought to write and tell you that the journey's not over yet. I have a Canadian friend whose drama class is using the piece for something and she shared it on her journal. It's a stunning piece. Definitely something I can relate to.

Marisa, South Africa

Back in 1986, my friend Cordula showed me "Bitte hoere, was ich nicht sage," a german translation of Please Hear What I'm Not Saying. This wonderful poem touched my soul and transformed my life forever thereafter.

F.H., Germany

This is an extremely touching and honest poem. I think its message is very important and I hope it will continue to help people around the world.

Elvy, Australia

I came across a line from "Please Hear" in an exchange that I will admit I likely should not have been privy to...Interestingly enough I discovered it to be reflective - like the last two lines read - of not only the person who had posted the line, but also of myself and likely many others. I will admit that I was not strong enough to continue to "beat down the walls" and ultimately was not the one who could "breathe life into this person"...but after reading the poem it gave me hope that the person whom I love still has shared it and someone in his world perhaps will "listen carefully and try to hear what (he's) not saying" and "that love is stronger than strong walls" and he will discover his own happiness and love.....in this lies my hope.

J, Canada

I just wanted to say that it's a really good poem and I forwarded it to all my friends and they all thought it was really good too and then when I read the history of the poem I found it amazing how it was passed on.

Emna, Egypt

It was probably the most beautiful thing that I have ever read—and I read a lot.

Susie, Spain

My mother, who was touched by the depth of your poem, recently sent me a copy of the first verse (the mask part) which was given to her by a friend and the author was assumed to be anonymous. Of course I immediately let my mum know that this was only a part of the poem and that there was indeed an author...Thank you again for resonating the love within human consciousness—it still continues to soften the calluses I have developed in a tough world.

Fara, British Columbia, Canada

I bought a second hand desk around 1987 and it was lying loose in a drawer. Alas, having found this site just last week, I see that I only got an abbreviated version, but I had circulated it to a few people on the net with whom I share a common interest. It is to be read out at my funeral.

George, UK

Thank you for this gift...a gift from heaven through your person.

Mariflor, Philippines

I am 25 years old and I struggle through some parts of life and I am on a journey to find myself. I thoroughly enjoyed the poem because different from most writings it says exactly how I feel about myself and people I am close to.

Susan, Australia

Again, repeating what everybody says, it touched me, though I read a version without the last two lines. So reading them kind of hit home, knowing that other people feel the same way. That I'm not the only person who goes through that sort of thing. I've always been wearing a 'mask' for as long as I can remember. I can remember times when I was 5 and a half when I used to pretend to be someone I wasn't. It's gotten worse and worse over the years as I've been exposed to more bad things and gotten more sensitive to spiritual things and reading this poem again made me feel... I don't know what the right word would be... It doesn't exactly fill me with a lot of hope, but, just contentment, I guess. I don't know if that's quite the right word. But it's the best I can think of right now.

Naomi, New South Wales, Australia

I appreciated your poem and it really touched me... Accidentally, I've read it when I really need help on facing my problems and I found everything on your poem.

Margaret, Philippines

In 1983 or 1984 3 youth (2 men Geof & Rod, 1 girl Sandi) preached a sermon in 2 churches in Western Australia. The topic was on love and nurture and caring for people. My friend Sandi read this poem...It is a timeless message that is very succinct and even more relevant now in the "postmodern" era where people only care for themselves at the expense of others...At 35 I was nearly killed in a car accident that left me with head injury and out of work permanently and that gave me a different (improved) view of the value of life and people. Before that I could not fully understand how people could pretend to be OK when they are not. Now I do that all the time myself. I'm in pain all the time, but people see me as fit and healthy because I am smiling and cheerful and helpful. But I do have many kind friends who encourage and pray for me often, which helps me survive life. And that is what your poem was for, to encourage us to look out for people whose "masks" hide a cry for help...

Geofrey, Australia

Such an incredible poem! The legacy you have created for yourself will no doubt abide in rich countless discriminating individuals for generations to come! Indeed I believe it to be a "litmus test" for identification of discerning human beings with a heightened capacity at deference to others, themselves, and the world about.

Avrohom, Israel

Thank you so much for this beautiful poem. I just posted it with a link to this website on my journal. It touched me because as a Christian I love to encourage those whose lives are hidden away and who are masked to the world. I want to share with them the love of Christ. So many times I get knocked back because they are hurting and it takes a long time to finally touch their inner spirit. But I know just as the poem says, Inside they are waiting for that love and hope of Christ to penetrate and bring them to life!! The life Christ has to give them!! I will pray that a special couple of people whom I have been praying for and encouraging for awhile come to read it.

Sharon, Victoria, Australia

Charles C. Finn

Thank you for being a gift to me.

Marie, New South Wales, Australia

I want to thank you for the beautiful words that make up this poem. I relate to the words so much and it explains exactly what I can't say. I am a survivor of childhood sexual abuse and your poem has been so inspiring since I first read it just a couple of months ago. It is a comfort to feel less alone.

May, UK

I was so grateful to find a place to express my gratitude for what this poem has meant to me over more than 30 years. I have never read anything that touched me more.

Cathie, Ontario, Canada

The poem screams SO MUCH truth! It is VERY clear that you must work with people in a "counsel" capacity.

Annelien, Johannesburg, South Africa

In the entire book "the child within" what connected and moved me the most was your poem. I sob, and sob, recognizing myself in it. Every night, before I go to bed, I read your poem to help me accept who I am, to heal my child within. I will share with my dear friends your marvelous piece…Merci.

P

The copy we found had a title of "Don't Be fooled by me." Wanting to know who wrote it, I Googled it and found the original. I love the simplicity of it, and how it has stuck a chord with all who read it. For the words are true for all who read it. I loved it.

John, Liverpool England

I love this poem.

Summer, Netherlands

Your poem was amazing.. It tells exactly how I feel right now. It made me cry. I dream of becoming a poet myself.

Jordan, New Brunswick, Canada

I stopped to listen to someone reading this out loud in a hospital ward. Powerful stuff, so much so that on my return to home, I looked it up to get a copy. Very good indeed, very accurate, will put a copy on my office wall so all the staff can read it and digest its meaning!

Gary, UK

Hello. It's amazing how a set of strung out words into a series of verses has had a huge impact on me and many others around the world. I came across this poem many many years ago and with the passage of time seemed to have forgotten about it until recently. I first came across it whilst being at school. I was heavily bullied as a child and neglected and abused at home. I read your poem out in a class assembly hoping that the teachers, the people who are supposed to take care of your well being whilst at school, would notice the sheer pain that I was in hiding behind a mask, words that I can not utter but through the use of a medium found ways to talk about what I felt. 15 years on I struggle to tell my therapist about how I feel so now having stumbled across this poem again, I'm just going to read it to him. It's simply beautiful how words can change a person, how they can melt a person, how they can bring hope and light to a darkened room.

Zaineb, UK

Chapter 6:
Creative Uses

Your poem has made a tremendous positive impact in my own life in dealing with others. It has helped me be gentler with my students and help create a safe classroom. Given that I have been using it in my role as a teacher of psychology since 1983 (including student teaching), I know that it has made a great impact on literally thousands of lives of my students...I have also shared it with other teachers at psychology teaching conferences in Indiana, Illinois and California. Thank you again for your humanity.

Chuck, California

I am an art therapist and have worked in the mental health field for over 10 years. I stumbled across your poem when I was a graduate student intern in an adult psychiatric hospital back in 1994. I fell in love with the poem and have lost count as to how many times I have utilized it in a group therapy discussion, in an individual session, and as a springboard into therapeutic art making of masks and various other metaphors my clients have been compelled to create in response to your poem...I will always hold onto this poem as a small treasure to offer my clients when they have difficulty finding their own words.

Michele

I have developed a program called Taking Back My Life. It is first designed for those incarcerated, in which they have an opportunity to review their entire life and see what changes they should make in their current belief system in order to make better choices in the future. We also work with their family members in hopes of a healthy reunification. This program will soon also be made available to anyone seeking personal growth and r recovery from one form of addiction or another. The main approach to discovering who they truly are is to get brutally honest and in doing so, begin to peel off the masks that they have hidden behind for so long. Your poem is perfect for this...I used to hide behind those masks of fear and did so with a bottle of vodka in my hand. Today I know personal freedom. We currently work with over 1400 US prisoners and many of their family members, as well as those in the community seeking recovery from addiction...I cannot tell you what it does to me to see a man who has served 25 years break down and cry, only to come back up after walking through the pain with restored hope and a renewed sense of self. This has been the most rewarding thing I have ever done in my life. I believe that the universe will lend its hand when the time is right and we will be able to reach many others who live in the middle of pain and fear.

Traci

I was one of many teens across Ohio attending a camp to learn more about drug prevention programs that we could take back to our schools and set up. The poem was delivered over the PA system and acted out by a Mime. This poem had a great impact on my life making me realize that everyone else had the same thoughts/fears as I...We had a high school theater student perform/recite this during a Town Hall Meeting on Underage Drinking just two years ago and I'm planning to get the poem to our current theater director for an in-school performance...I think this should be required reading for high school students everywhere.

Susie, Ohio

I am co-leader of a support group for Rape Crisis and had told them last week of your poem and that I would bring it this week. A friend of mine in high school (1982) had a notebook filled with poems she liked, and had let me borrow it. When I gave it back she asked if I had read the really long one. I said no I hadn't. She gave it back and told me to read it. I am glad that she did. It is one of the most profound poems I have ever read. I have passed it on to people many times. There were a few parts that I thought must have gotten lost in translation so tonight I looked it up on the internet and found your site. I am very happy to have found the complete version and its story. I loved the poem because I saw myself in it. But I loved the end because it gave me comfort in knowing that I was not alone, everyone felt that way. I think knowing that everyone felt that way made me able to open up and reach out to other people the way that I hoped people would reach out to me. Thank you for a poem that not only touched my life but opened me up to touch other people's lives.

Traci, Ohio

Hi. Sorry, I don't know very well English. I am clinical psychologist in Turkey. Firstly, I met with your poem in a book in 1992. I trained art therapy from 2004 to 2009. I used your poem in communication groups for health staff. We used expressive art therapy with the patients who has breast cancer diagnosis. This poem is very good.

Birgul, Turkey

I am a School Psychologist...I have to let you know that I first came upon your poem when I was about 20 years old working in an adolescent treatment center...I used that poem often to initiate discussion in our group therapies for emotionally disturbed adolescents. I then went on to work in an elementary school in Milwaukee and spent some time in juvenile corrections work as well. Your poem was able to help many young people let their guard down, open up, and really talk about what was going on with them. Through all of the frustration of working in this field, your poem helped me to keep going and keep believing in the importance of the work we do. And, as you state so eloquently, it was not just them but myself who was able to benefit by doing some soul searching also.

Becky, Wisconsin

My sophomore high school English teacher presented the Poem to me after several long personal conversations. He was an amazing man. He had a way about him that made you feel as if you weren't just a kid.... he made you feel "special." I had a great deal going on underneath the tide and without saying a word he understood. I was out to prove myself to the world and to be better than anyone else. The poem touched me deeply. I have never forgotten it and I have referenced it too many times to count. I still have the copy he gave to me and I have shared it with several people along my life's journey. I have worked in Holistic medicine for over 20 years and I have shared your poem with clients along that path as well. I have recently returned to school and the head of the program I am in and I have had several chats around the psychosocial aspect working with clients and being attentive to what they are not saying, so again I found myself referring back to your poem.

Desiree, Oregon

Attending my undergrad studies at Buffalo, one of my roommates pulled out a 'version' of this original poem. Someone in one of her classes had used it as part of a project. She was moved by it, made a copy for herself, and shared it with me and our other roommate. I too was very moved by it and made a copy for myself as well. There was no 'author' on it. I've kept it for years, and eventually came across another 'version' of it in one of the many "Chicken Soup for the Soul" books, again, no author. This time, I had since graduated with my Master's in Social Work - Family Mental Health, and have very often used this as a teaching tool with many of my clients. Many had also been moved to tears upon reading it, both teens and adults alike.

Greeneyezz, New York

I just wanted to say how impressed I have been by your poem. I first came upon it while working with the Division of Youth Services in Missouri. It was used in treatment in residential settings. I don't know who began it, but I was the one who dissected, so to speak, so that other workers could present the poem to the group. Most often it really makes our kids bounce off the walls. It spoke to the kids, and to us who were dealing with them. For those of us who never walked the life of our residents, it taught them not to personalize when a kid became belligerent or angry. It made them understand that we are onions, that there are many layers to us…I still use this poem with the kids I work with.

Kristen, Missouri

Hi, I found the 'Masks' version of the poem about five years ago and have been using it with clients in my counseling practice, and in creative training workshops for counselors. I used it with a client yesterday and he has just emailed me to tell me you had written it, and I am thrilled to know its true story and history! Thanks you so much - your words have helped many clients I have worked with.

Sarah, England

Thank you for the perfect poem. This poem means more today than it did years ago when I first read it. I will be giving it to my best friend in the hopes it will give her a better understanding of where I am right now and also to my current counselor to use with his other patients. Again thank you for giving those of us a voice when we just couldn't seem to do it ourselves.

Diane, Missouri

I'm planning to use it at a retreat for women in March. Thank you for a timely expression of universal aloneness.

Frieda, North Carolina

I was introduced to your poem in October 1976 while attending an Air Force school for alcohol and drug counselors in San Antonio, Texas… Your poem was one of the first tools we were introduced to in the beginning of a ten day intensive psychotherapy training group in which we knew we were going to be monitored and graded…After some basic introductions our facilitator asked us to turn our chairs about. Said that he wanted us to focus on ourselves for a moment because it might be the last opportunity for us to do that for awhile with what we were about to embark upon. Told us to pick a spot on the wall and stare at it until it was no longer in focus all the while suggesting we think about the reasons we were there at that moment in time. His smooth, calm, reassuring tone was almost hypnotic in nature as he proceeded to have us relax even more by closing our eyes and concentrating on various muscles in our bodies, working from foot to head, which very effectively had us, at least me for sure, focusing on just ME. As he brought the focus to the top of our heads he told us to relax our breathing even more and just listen to the words he was about to read—which of course was your poem, to which I, and I can probably safely say everyone else, thought had been drafted just for them. The poem as a tool was used like a key to open the minds, hearts and souls of all who attended in preparation for the process of sharing and feedback that were to follow, so that none would think that they were any more or less secure in their humanness than the next. That key to awareness was instrumental in opening my eyes that day in October and resulted in my decision to marry after sharing your poem with my girlfriend at the time and now my wife of almost 30 years. I went on to use that poem in countless counseling sessions, both individual and group; never having to worry about whether it would generate feelings, emotions or discussion that generally led to positive growth in those whose lives it touched, like mine.

Bob, Texas

I now teach graduate classes in counseling and always use the poem.

Jarrell, South Carolina

I had emailed this poem to Dorothy V. who will be using this in her devotional sometime...She helps a lot of abused children...Thank you for touching my heart and my life and also my family's life.

Cathy, Oklahoma

Thanks for such a deep insight into human nature. I am using this poem in my college courses for social work.

Kim, Wisconsin

Your poem is an excellent introduction to the world of therapeutic communication and will be read to my students.

Lylia, Pennsylvania

The crazy thing about this poem is that soon after reading it, I found myself talking to others about it and seeing that it may have just been the thing they needed to hear, myself included. I have found that this is the paradigm in which we need to view people, from a place of nonjudgement and a place to give them a chance. These are words that our world needs right now. I have shared your poem with several people I work with as with some of my family. All have found your words inspiring. I work as a corporate trainer and have found that this poem identifies with many people, both on a professional and personal level.

Candace, Kansas

I am part of a large (mega) church in Plymouth MI. As part of giving back to the community, NorthRidge Church offers "LifeShare" groups that provide support and recovery from hurts and issues of life. "A safe place for hope and healing." My group deals with "compulsive overeating" and Charlie's poem was shared last night in class. Thank you so much for this poem of help and hope!

Stephen, Michigan

I was moved by this poem the first time I heard it back in the 1980's and still today get chills each and every time I read it. I now teach psychology and I often read it to my students. I asked my students if any of them knew who the author was. One of the students took it upon himself to do a search and came back with this website. "Please Hear What I'm Not Saying" is a treasured piece of writing I have kept all these years and have probably read it hundreds of times.

Susan, Michigan

I teach a drama/clowning class at a small private school. We have junior high and high school students I will share your poem with.

Sharon, Texas

A portion of your poem was given to me years ago. I felt as if it had been written specifically about me. It was everything I felt and wished I could say. At that time in my life I could not express myself. I am a survivor of childhood sexual abuse and the poem came to me at an extremely difficult time in my life. As my website expands I am in the process of creating pages in which I hope to assist other abuse victims claim back their lives.

Joanne, Massachusetts

I have used this poem over and over to solidify my point when I teach on human suffering. I now have a ministry with the homeless. This poem has helped me convey a strong message to ignorant citizens within our communities expressing "we all hide behind masks." Thank you so much...I read it over and over to remind me of the frailty of human suffering. It also reminds me that we all hold the wonders of hope for others needing compassion, understanding.

Pamela, Alberta, Canada

My friend Sandi and her husband David visit a prison each week with spiritual programs to encourage and nurture the prisoners, and help them gain some self esteem despite their often horrible childhood and youth experiences. She said your poem will be of use in helping the prisoners be open in communicating and sharing their feelings and emotions with people who genuinely care about their well being.

Geofrey, Australia

In all the years my parents were heavily involved with Marriage Encounter groups, they used your poem in many ways.

Meredith, Washington, DC

I'm a first year Theatre and Performance student from the University of Leeds, England. One of our modules for this year includes one called "Collaboration." After six weeks of training a group of us are given a box with different materials from which to devise a performance. One of the stimuli we were provided with was the title of your poem, and I went away to research it and found the full length copy on your web page. It's a wonderful poem and it really spoke to me. I'm taking it into our group session tomorrow and I hope it'll have the same impact on them and I hope also that it will have a major influence on our performance. It's a great poem to be able to work from because it contains so many human emotions and tons of ideas have come to my head already...I thought I'd let you know your poem is still traveling and reaching people.

Holly, UK

I have been familiar with your poem since I discovered it in a handbook from a treatment center for substance abuse in Denver. A patient I had referred there brought it back to me. It continues to ring true and is a useful tool to provoke personal growth, genuineness and self-acceptance.

Roger, Virginia

We used the text of "Please Hear What I'm Not Saying" in my Acting II course last semester at Westmont College in Santa Barbara, CA to formulate a performance art piece for our Fringe Festival...We were really inspired by the piece and loved using it. We connected the ideas of the monastic principles of St. Benedict with the idea of masks.

Chandra, California

I was a new English teacher who had created a new course with two other teachers in 1975. The idea of the course was to address the needs of students in an interdisciplinary course...Your poem was brought to us by a student (unfortunately without your name) and we used it as a part of our unit "Love, Loneliness, and Alienation" for 25 years...I am reviving it today as I begin my second career as a teacher all over again. It speaks to our young people and causes them to think and write.

Michael, Indiana

Chapter 7:
Relating to Youth

I came across this poem when I was a teen. The idea that "mask wearing" might be universal, and not just my personal weakness/ failure, was a profound paradigm shift for me. Working with "at risk" teens today, this poem came to mind, and I can attest that it has lost none of it power to touch lives. For over thirty years I have anonymously thanked the anonymous poet. I am thrilled to be given the opportunity to publicly acknowledge and show my gratitude for your fine poem.

Kathleen, Oklahoma

I first read the poem around my freshman year in high school, 1986. I truly at that young of an age had made it my own to the point where I thought I had written it, so in turmoil was my life, so much did I need something of my own expressing how I felt. Honestly, your writing put into words all the things I was feeling that at the age of 14 or 15 I could never figure out how to articulate. I have kept it in a box of high school memorabilia all these years. No matter what inspired you to write that poem, I am sure you never dreamed that a 14-year-old despondent girl in a small town in Missouri in such a dysfunctional, codependent repressed home would come across something you wrote before she was born and attach herself to it so wholly that it would lay bare her soul and give her words she never had to identify those feelings inside of her that she could never tell anyone. I believe that God touched me through you without you even knowing it.

Valerie, Illinois

I was a very angst-filled, depressed teenager. I wasn't into drinking or drugs, but I did have chronic depression, with some spiritual warfare thrown in to boot. I was in church Sunday, and the pastor read this during his sermon. The only change he made (I got a copy from him) was to add the line, "I am sitting right beside you," to the poem, and I believe that was because we were in the church, sitting. I remember sitting there, tears streaming down my cheeks, wondering how he knew me so well. I was sitting very quietly so as not to give myself away as he read...I didn't want everyone else to know it was me that he was talking about. Till he got to the last two lines. So many people have no idea that everyone else out there feels the same way they do. That we're all just as uncertain and unsure of ourselves as the next person. If only they could remember that, perhaps we'd treat each other a little more kindly.

Cookiebear, Washington

I was in the seventh grade when I was given a copy of this poem. It was so important to me that I would carry it around with me for the next five years. I lost it eventually. I kept looking for it but couldn't find the exact version until I found this site. You see, I suffered from depression and in the seventh grade is when I began to hide my feelings, through self-injury. I began to hurt myself to hide the fact that I was hurting on the inside - hurting from the abuse I was suffering by the hands of my brother and that I did suffer by the hands of my next door neighbor. It wouldn't be until I was 23 years old that I would come to terms with it and take of this pervasive mask that was so strong. Thank you for telling this poem - it told my story.

Amanda, New York

It was 1983, and I was a thirteen-year old who'd just been admitted to a private psychiatric hospital in Skokie, IL. I was scared, overwhelmed and overcome with emotion. After thirteen years of growing up in different families...and not having a real dad, I was a sad and confused young girl. I'd always put on a happy face, been a model student, successful and involved in tons of activities, a happy girl who greeted everyone and helped others. But I was hiding the fact that I struggled with childhood depression. Until then, I didn't even know my feelings and struggles had a name, diagnosis, or treatment.

One special and my favorite staff member, Ann, handed out this poem in November of 1983; I was in my second month of what would be a five-month stay at this hospital. Though it was handed out to all the kids, I felt like it was speaking directly to me. I'd never read anything that put my feelings into words so perfectly. The jig was up—I was unhappy, and this poem made me feel I wasn't alone.

In the following months and through that long winter at, I learned how to be happy again. I finally shared my feelings, talked things through with my mom and saw a future that would be happy and successful and secure.

A year later, I would use this poem as my monologue in acting auditions for Chicago's High School for the Arts. I got in.

In summary, this poem changed my life. It had the right words at the right time, and was what I needed to open up to people and begin to become real. Thank you!

Erin, Maryland

I was very touched as a sixteen year old when I first heard the poem. I have been a teacher since the age of twenty and have used the poem as inspiration for my interactions with students, staff and parents.

Paul, Ontario, Canada

Just to say thank you for the poem. It touched me in a deep way when I first heard it as a teenager 11 years ago. I have subsequently referred to it many times in youth ministry, and find it portrays the importance of deep, listening relationships very well. Relationships in the teenage years are becoming a passion of mine, and I shall probably continue to use it in my training, to try and push the importance home of being a true listener and a carer. Thank God, I now know who the author is.

Andy, South Africa

You wrote your poem 45 years ago, but today's teenagers enjoy in that. And I'm sure it will be the same after next 45 years. This poem is for all humanity. Everybody in this world is going through all these feelings, somewhere, sometimes. That "mask wearing" idea is universal, and not just my personal weakness. You found a way to write those feelings down on paper and we are very thankful for that!

Isidora, Bosnia and Herzegovina

It's so good to be able to get to know the author of this wonderful poem I came across thirty years ago! I was a school girl of 15, now 45, when my Literature teacher gave this to the class for critical appreciation lesson. I was 15, confused about all the issues of youth, love, friendship, relationships, drugs, alcohol and what have you. I found a solace in that poem which has resonated with me so much. I have not stopped sharing it with friends, relatives and my four children.

Ai-ming, Singapore

I have been deeply touched by and have loved your poem since my days of childhood, and probably have a copy in my childish handwriting somewhere. Your poem was one of the first things that inspired me, as were the poems of Kahlil Gibran. I have shared it with many people in the "uniquely Me" seminars that I've taught over the years to groups of adults, children and teens...I honor your muse...Here's the response of a friend I sent it to: "This is a beautiful poem that a friend mailed me from a land almost ten hours behind us. I found it enchanting. I found it truthful. I found it honest. And I definitely found it real. Some of you may not like reading poems, but here I request you to take some time off and read this poem. Probably read it loud enough so that you can hear the words throbbing your ears. At the end of your reading, if you find the poem meaningful and peaceful, please pass it on. It will surely do your world, and the world at large, a world of good."

Dayu, Florida

I was young and found it very difficult to express myself. I was battling some fairly severe depression and my parents finally put me into therapy.

I would disappoint myself every week at our visits because I would refuse to really talk and I would feel like a failure each time I exited. I felt like I was a coward, afraid of letting anyone see the real me. My Mom bought me the "Chicken Soup for the Teenage Soul" book. I read it and really enjoyed many of the entries, but never felt a TRUE connection with any... until, I came upon your poem. I believe it was labeled "masks." It touched me so deeply. I felt like, this WAS me. I brought it into my counselor because I felt I could offer a glimpse of me this way. He read it and asked me a few things about it. He then set up a meeting with my parents and my younger sister and had me read it to them aloud. There were many long sobbing pauses and tons of true tears, but I somehow made it through. My parents were shocked saying that they never knew I felt that way. I said I was just very good at wearing my masks. I was so thankful for your poem and it really was a pivotal moment in my life. I must say, when reading this as a young adult, I was not expecting those last two lines. I was a bit relieved in feeling as if I wasn't the only person like this. While at the same time, I wanted it to be me and only me, so people could understand me better. I wanted to strike them out and write, "I am your daughter." I was speaking about that to my husband last night and when I came to work today I felt compelled to find a copy of that poem. I found myself feeling just as vulnerable as I did as a child and just as tearful!

Sara, Missouri

Glad to find an "old friend" here! I recited this poem for speech class in high school, in 1991, and was chosen to give it in front of the school assembly. As a shy, new transfer student, I felt heartened by it, tried to remember this in all my interactions with others. I still know it by heart. Thanks for comforting a lonely high school student, and continuing to inspire me now.

Rose, Pennsylvania

I have had an abbreviated version of your poem since a Girl Guide leadership training in 1987 (it does however have the last lines!). I would love to use it in a program sheet for Girl Guides in Victoria to help leaders of Guides 13+ find an activity to help them open up discussions around self esteem, self worth, how the girls are feeling about themselves, and to celebrate their confidences.

Merilyn, Australia

I have recently discovered your poem…I must say reading it gave me a little twinge because this poem was honest and very vivid. I myself am a writer. I am only 16 years old but I have ambition. I just wanted to thank you for your beautiful poem, it gives writers like me hope. The poem talked about wearing a mask. For a while I kinda was. You see my friend thinks that writers are worthless bums that won't amount to anything. She almost convinced me to consider changing career paths but thanks to your beautiful poem I thought differently. Because your poem taught me how to be comfortable in my own skin. I've always dreamt of being a writer some day but I guess I never really came to terms with it till now.

Christianna

Your poem has touched my son's life very deeply. He's been a troubled kid all his life and is in a place in his life where he has to get control and try to understand himself and the "whys" of his life. For you to have written something so profoundly remarkable that it touches lives deeply for so many years…Thank you for opening a door to my son's soul.

Tess, Pennsylvania

I heard this poem and never forgot it because it told the story of my soul as an 8th grader. Very smart, but not too popular - 10th child of 12; very little or no self-worth, verbose, chip on my shoulder, yet wanting so much to be loved - afraid to be who I really was…. you said it all. Fast-forward, I started a ministry, "FASHION with GRACE", a fashion and charm class with 30+ students now, ages 12-18 in Detroit; I teach them to sew, do crafts, life-skills, bible-based principles for life and most of all, that they have intrinsic value, that they are loved and have something unique and exciting to offer to God, to themselves and to the world. I googled this poem to see if I could still find it, having no idea that it was so popular but I can see why; as it says, it is everybody we meet. I was these girls, and I'm doing all I can to help them to see one of the greatest things that has helped to change my life - That God loves me just the way I am, and it's okay to be me. Through that revelation I have been able to take off my mask - hopefully I will help them remove theirs. I plan to share and discuss this powerful poem with them in our next semester.

Jean, Michigan

I had read the poem Please Hear What I'm Not Saying when I was in high school (I'm 33 yrs old now). I've had a rough life, and my English teacher had given this poem to me. This poem has meant so much more to me. I wrote a ton of poetry throughout my life, and your poem enabled me to express what was inside, even if it was just through poetry, since I have a hard time talking about all the trauma and abuse I have been through as a child, and still go through as an adult, the poem means so much to me.......and I see it in those who are in my life, struggling also...I've shared it w/ them, I don't know if anyone has told you thank you so much for deeply affected their lives, but I want to tell you that from the bottom of my heart and let you know, because you shared your inner most emotions with the world, people have been enabled to embrace and share the pain, express themselves better, know there are people out there just like us.

Suzanne, PA

I am in 8th grade, and have now joined the speech team...In two more days I will be going to another tournament, I hope to get a ribbon then with your wonderful poem. The first time that I looked over your poem I got chills up my spine, this poem is SO powerful.

Ashley

I was looking for a piece I could perform and I wanted something to say "hey, this is my life, this poem is just like me," and there it was. I love it so much, no, it is my life now. I think it rules. It is just like me, like it was made for me!!!!!!!!!!!!!!!!!!!!!!!!

Cierra, Texas

I can remember back to when my mother read this poem in front of our church. Sitting in the sanctuary I can remember how the words sank in. There was complete silence during that time; you could hear a pin drop. Fourteen years later, I have the opportunity to read something of my choice as part of an assignment in my Voice and Articulation class. This poem was what first came to mind.

Susan, Oregon

I pulled this poem out so I can share it with a 7th and 8th grade youth group. It has had an impact on me.

Michelle, Nebraska

Thank you for such a wonderful poem. It is sad that the significance of the message has not been picked up by many in all these years. It has been 40 years since the poem was written and more than ever it pertains to today's children and young persons, and old for that matter. Parents, educators, and society cannot assume that older kids do not need our attention, guidance and love…

Sara

I honestly can't recall when was the first time I've encountered this poem, but the first time it really struck me was when I attended the youth encounter seminar workshop in our parish. During the first session the poem was read to us. At first it was just like "oh! That's great!" They gave us a copy of that poem and during our break I read it again. As I was reading it alone, I don't know why suddenly tears flow from my eyes. It went directly to my system. It's as if I was the one who wrote it telling the world, "Hey world, can you listen to what I am NOT saying?!" I am a happy person and people viewed me as someone strong and a happy go lucky, but they don't know what really lies behind, and this is what the poem is telling. After that, I have learned to always read between the lines. I've always been my friends' friend and confidante. This poem had inspired me to not judge but to look deeper because definitely there might be something different going on. It helped me to understand other people.

Sharon, Philippines

While attending high school in 1970 in New York, my then girlfriend Michelle gave it to me during class. It was hand printed and folded up. I have always treasured it and kept the original copy in my fire safe. Every time I read it, I feel it more. I have always shared it and will continue to do so.

Armando, Florida

In high school, in lieu of learning Sci-Fi, I convinced my English teacher to allow me the opportunity to study poetry. In the universes whirling magical way, I came upon your famous poem…It was the poem I chose to learn, thus recite to the class. I did not know, back in 1976, what this poem held for me. Locked away, safely aware these words were a shield that would save me, yes, save my life. Years, years 1989, I would discover I was a multiple of mind; today they call it Dissociative Identity Disorder. My mind literally shattered to make space for all the atrocities an 8 year old girl could not handle, register, feel, as a forced member of a satanic cult. I share this because, as a non-published writer, we wonder—on those silent days of fumbling for the "it" word, do we really make a difference. I can say you certainly have in my life…The pages are yellowed, the verses underlined, parenthesis defining what I needed to learn to hear in your words kept me going. Knowing others have felt the mask of life…Knowing the Mask as okay, though mine a bit deeper in explanation, I viewed my movement through life just a Mask until I felt safe enough to allow me to be me.

Meg

I was around 13 (15 years ago) when I first heard this poem. I was attending youth prayer meetings and a family friend used to give me rides to the meetings. One night, for some reason that I can't now recall, he told me about this poem and recited it to me from memory. I was astounded that he had memorized such a long poem. The poem really did strike a chord in me at that time. I had ALWAYS felt like I was 'wearing a mask' and that very few people knew the 'real' me…I am teaching an Intro Psych course right and we are now beginning the section on personality. Our textbook mentions how the word 'personality' comes from the latin 'persona' which translates to 'masks.' This all triggered a memory of the poem ("I wear a mask, a thousand masks")...I think the poem has made many people feel as I did— comforted by the idea that I was not the only one who felt alone sometimes and wore a thousand masks.

Theresa, Massachusetts

I copied the poem and distributed it to 7th and 8th graders in the school where I was interning. It had a powerful effect on many. I have always kept a copy handy. Just today, I sent it to a good friend who is struggling with addiction and parole.

Bob, Pennsylvania

This poem was very inspirational to me. As a thirteen year old girl, I read it, and knew it was meant for me. It was everything that I needed to hear. It definitely had a large impact on my life. It touched me and shaped who I am today.

Tonya, North Carolina

My 8th grade teacher gave it out to us. This is my favorite poem of all time. It has a place of honor on the back of my door, where only the most important things in my life are placed.

Emily, Georgia

Here's how I heard about the poem (and I've been using it for nearly 40 years). Young Life, a Christian youth organization for high school kids published it in a magazine in the late 60's. It was attributed to an 11th grade student from Bismark, ND. I've been using the poem in its entirety in my teaching for nearly 40 years!

Jack, Pennsylvania

I first came in contact with your poem on a youth retreat in the Episcopal Diocese of Texas called "Happening." This poem was and is a show stopper that made an impact on me then and to this day. I know that most of the other attendees and my friends had the same impression made on them as well. The Happening weekend is now a nationwide program with the talk "Please Hear What I'm Not Saying" as the opening talk. I thought you would find it interesting to know how it has permeated into the religious realm.

Richard, Texas

As a young man in West Texas, I experienced an Episcopal Youth Event called "Happening," where I had first heard your poem. The following year, I was asked to deliver this beautiful message at another Happening event...The words are so vulnerable, very real, and its truth of persona struck me in a positive way. My walls are still strong, but with lots of windows.

Michael, Texas

This is my favourite poem. Has been since I first came across it while searching on the Internet for something to make me feel better. I was 13 years old, feeling very confused about who I was and feeling very alone in the world. I read this poem and realised that others felt the same way I did and that made me feel not so alone.

Victoria, England

I first heard about this poem when I was walking out of the office at my old middle school. School had just gotten out, so there was a rush for the door. When I walked out, I noticed that someone had dropped a folded up paper. Out of curiosity I picked it up and unfolded it. I began to read, and couldn't put the paper down. Sure it was crinkled and desecrated, but I kept it. It fit with what was happening in my life at that point in time. I fell in love with the poem, and made almost everyone read it...I just wanted to say that this poem makes me feel at home, and is very true to what many people are going through. I believe that it has a great message and should be widely known.

Meghan, California

I was struggling to come up with a piece for my forensics tournament, and I had asked my mother what would be a good poem and she referred me to this poem. She said she didn't know if I was actually going to be able to find it but when I found I was so excited I paired this poem with John Denver's song Rhymes and Reasons, and I took first place at my tournament. I had comments such as this poem was so inspirational. Thank you for creating such a master piece that I will take with me for the rest of my life.

Lexy, Wisconsin

What a touching poem, so meaningful, especially for teens. Sorry I did not read it earlier in life but glad that I found it, or it found me. I can see why it has been so often borrowed.

Judy, Virginia

For many years before I read this poem, I had been writing poetry. When I entered High School, my Freshman English teacher allowed me to do a 10 minute journal and he also read a lot of my poems. He gave me a copy of "Please Hear What I'm Not Saying" to help me understand how I was feeling and it was so perfect. At one point, my family thought I wrote it.

Kathleen, Texas

I first learned about this poem in rehab and I loved it. I am not big into poetry but I will never forget this poem. Now I am in college and will be writing a reaction paper to the poem.

Wendy, Oregon

So I guess this poem was written a very long time ago but I just discovered it today when looking for a poem for a class assignment. I just want to say that your poem really brings to life the struggle that almost everyone experiences but no one talks about. I felt as though the poem could have been written exactly for me and then after I sent the poem to a couple others they said the exact same thing. I have read it over and over and every time it brings tears to my eyes but is also refreshing to read.

Alison, Indiana

I'm happy to hear a name attached to the "anonymous" voice that spoke to me for so long. I first received this poem in 1977, as a seventh grader, in a writing workshop. It stayed with me, as I read it aloud as a "presentation" to my tenth grade English class in 1980, then again at a "talent show" in college, 1983. Came up tonight as a student of mine referenced an Emily Dickinson poem ("I'm nobody") and the comment drew me back to "...every man you meet... every woman you meet. " Stunning work.

Kim

Chapter 8:
Relating to Substance Abuse/Addiction

I heard this poem at the lowest possible time in my life. I was 21 with a raging addiction to meth and no hope. This poem seemed like it had been what I was trying to say in so many negative ways. I believe it made all the difference in my life. I have since become a counselor for troubled youth and now a teacher for non credit classes at a local college. I work with young kids all the time and eventually, this poem becomes part of the lessons. I know it has touched some of my students as much as it has touched me.

Jodi, Iowa

I just want to thank you after all these years for your poem. I first heard it read in a rehab for alcoholism in Maine in 1987. I was there as a supporting family member only to find myself in my own rehab in January of 1988 for alcoholism. Your poem was instrumental in opening my eyes to the truth of my life, and it started me on a long journey of recovery from myself. Now twenty years later I have pulled that poem out once again to share with others who like myself are recovering from food addiction. Thank you for following the leadings of your heart and jotting down a few lines that are transcending time and still touching lives today. I wear fewer masks today because of your poem.

Catharine, Maine

I was first introduced to "Please Hear What I Am Not Saying" from a youth counselor. I read it and immediately connected with it. It has been almost 14 years since I have laid eyes on this poem but it has always been on a part of me. As a recovering addict, it gives me a deep spiritual uplifting and reminds me to be true to self and to always remain at the service of others.

Brian, Alaska

As a substance abuse counselor, I have used this poem many times as a teaching tool, working with incarcerated men faced with chronic substance abuse/numerous arrests in substance abuse units. The poem was read and discussed, and the meaning explored. The men made their own masks (real and pretend) and wearing them, they opened up and faced the truth of who they were, honestly, in front of the others. The results were men who saw themselves differently, without shame, for the first time.

Sara, Texas

I'm a 54 year old recovering alcoholic. My AA sponsor gave me a copy of this poem and I still have it, but today it was time to pass it on to another friend (I've done so many times). Thank you for helping me and so many others not feel alone. This poem just sticks with you and comes back when you need it the most.

Susan, Colorado

I read your poem in 1976 when I was at a drug/alcohol rehab in New Jersey. I've been in AA for 28 years and keep active sponsoring other recovering women. It's what keeps me growing and sober. Please Hear was powerful and identified a part of my soul that was ready to be recognized and loved.

Cathy

Some years ago I was working as a social worker with addicts. It was the most fulfilling job I ever had. Not easy, you can imagine, but whenever I think of those days, my heart fills with love. It made me stronger, it made me who I am, even when I was trying to find myself as well…Boy, was it hard at first. The people I had to teach differed in age from 15 to 50, roughly. And they had been working together, without anyone to teach them, for a long time. So I had to earn my presence, had to earn my leadership. It was tough.

Several people I was coaching kept a place in my heart. There was one lady, who was extremely difficult for me. One day she could be sweet beyond belief, the next day she could be aggressive, fight, have psychotic moments. A real challenge to be in contact with her. But one day, she entered the room, gave me a piece of paper and said: "Take it, read it please…" Of course I did. It was a translation of your poem, Please hear what I'm not saying. Needless to say, I was moved. And surprised. From her??? We looked into each other's eyes and really saw each other at that moment. For one moment we were one. And although she remained a challenge to handle, we knew each other and it was ok…I am fortunate in that I have several very close friends, who see me for who I am, deep down inside. I cherish every one of them, and often tell them about your poem. Your poem says it all.

Ilonka, The Netherlands

I read this as a teen and knew the author must have written it about my feelings. I went to treatment and am now a counselor, sober over 20 years. I still use this poem in my groups with recovering individuals.

Michelle, Arizona

This poem came to me in the most vulnerable time in my life when I knew I needed help. It said everything I could not say. It helped me say what I needed to say. After I began the recovery process, I continued to use that very poem before I gave any talks for meetings or special occasions. Of late, I relapsed emotionally, and only came to realize where I was when I felt myself wanting to disappear again. For days, I put all my recovery tools into place, willing to be so very honest with myself and another and God, and I am now on the pathway into recovery again from the past several months of relapse. Thank God for the inspiration of this poem.

Cindy, Texas

This poem is the story of my life before I quit consuming alcohol. I have been sober for 23 years but do not forget the many masks a person can wear to hide their pain. This poem is quite different from wearing different hats (my counselor hat, my mother hat, my sister hat, my friend hat).

Janie, Michigan

I came across this poem today as I was sorting through some of my readings and writings on recovery work. This is so beautiful and poignant that it brought me to tears, once again.

Joan, Pennsylvania

This poem so describes me for the 28 years I spent using drugs and alcohol, after being sexually abused by my biological father as a teen, but today I'm finally free.

Deborah, Alaska

A teacher read this poem in class one day when I was 15 years old. It absolutely touched me at that time and I have held onto it all these years—I practically had it memorized word-for-word! Now I am in recovery for a drug addiction and this poem came to mind…I am going to read it on my graduation day from my intensive outpatient group therapy.

Michele, Indiana

I absolutely love this poem. I sat at my table after going through old files and memorabilia from a very difficult time in my life with drugs and alcohol and bawled my eyes out reading your poem…Thank you for everything I could not say.

Barbara, Michigan

I was 4 years sober at the time and was able to read this from a stage in front of 4000 AA members as I was crying. The words were lost to me for over 30 years. 2 weeks ago as if by a miracle I was able to find the first words in my life (at the time) that expressed my deepest and most hidden feelings. THANK YOU!!!

Louie, California

How wonderful to finally learn who-and-where this poem originated. I share it with all my 'sponsees.'

Karl, Colorado

I am a recreation therapist at a drug rehab facility in Hoffman Estates. This poem was given to me from a clinician and suggested I use it as a tool with my "mask" projects. Excellent poem.

Marcy, Illinois

I quit drinking 1998 and soon began seeing a therapist/counselor. Her name is Anne and I saw her, with varying frequency, until I moved from Arizona to North Carolina at the beginning of 2007. She was instrumental (along with AA) in helping me grow, learn to accept myself, become strong and to live without fear. During one of the early years of our work together, probably after repeating for the umpteenth time about my low self-esteem, she gave me a copy of this poem. I could not believe how well it reflected how I felt. I have kept it on my cork board and still get goosebumps when I read it.

Diane, North Carolina

I love this poem because it describes my whole life, life as an alcoholic, and the mind-games I play with myself and other people; so afraid of failure. So many recovering alcoholics and drug addicts wear the same masks, masks that they are afraid to take off for fear of not being accepted. Page 417 (449, Older Version) of the AA Big Book is about Acceptance. After being able to accept life as the way it is supposed to be at the moment, I could remove those masks that I wore for all these years.

Sam, North Carolina

While in the US Army at the Presidio during 1973-77 it was 'passed around' to a group of counselors at the Alcohol and Drug Abuse

Prevention and Control Program (Whew!). I next saw it in about 1996 as the work of a 14 year old student at Mitchell High School in Colorado Springs, CO (my daughter said the student got class credit for it as her own creation!). This morning it suddenly surfaced in my thoughts as 'Don't Be Fooled By Me'. I Googled it (Happy Day!) and was rewarded by what I believe to be the original copy by C. C. Finn. At age 80 it has been an inspiration to me for over 30 years.

Bill, New York

I love this poem and have done it as a dramatic oral reading in churches, as part of a teaching tool in educating about the homeless. All of us wear masks, but addicts wear more of them, and they wear them tighter to their face.

Michele, Nova Scotia

I don't remember how, when, or where I found it. I just know that it spoke to my heart. I have felt this way before, for many years of my life. I know others have too. It is truly every man and every woman. I am a recovering codependent, and this poem could very easily be named the "fight song" for codependency. Thank you for letting it flow from your heart to paper and out to the world.

Serenity

Chapter 9:
Relating to Suicide

Years ago in the late 70's I was going through therapy, divorce and early family issues. I was suicidal and wanted to die, thought I had lost everything and did not know how to continue. My therapist gave me your poem. I read it and something clicked inside of me. I had some understanding about myself and the mask I wore all of my life. I also began to see how other folks also hid behind their masks. It made a change in my life then and upon reading it again at your website made me think again about that time and how it helped me get where I am today. Thank you for helping me find my life!

Bill

I read this poem years ago when I was in the hospital because I wanted to die from a childhood of abuse but especially sexual abuse. So I wanted to thank you because it helped me many years ago to come out from behind some masks and be healed by allowing others to gradually get closer to me and accept love and care from a few. It was the love of my granny that also kept me alive.

Rebeccah, Arizona

I was 14 years old when at church camp they gave us this poem. I was deep in depression with suicidal thoughts. The poem grabbed my heart, someone understood me. I was hurt, alone, scared, hiding behind all the masks I could muster—someone understood. I carried that poem with me to adulthood, somehow I found some sanity in it. Over the years I have had to retype it as the papers wore out, and I shared it with many people because it made sense to me. Today I am 50, depression and suicide free. I still think this poem makes sense to me, it was and is me.

Jeannette, Florida

In 1992 I was in treatment for a suicide attempt and depression. I was saved by what someone once told me was "A God's Deal." With her help and that hand that she held out I took hold. She gave me that Poem and it's gotten me though difficult times in life. I don't know where she is anymore, but the poem hangs on my wall and I look at it when times get hard. And I hear her voice and the words that saved my life. SHE HEARD WHAT I WAS NOT SAYING.

Velvet, Texas

I bet you hear this a lot, but that poem is me. Everything about it fit my life to a T. This poem has been something that I have kept with me throughout my life journey. Even though I am only 39 your poem had brought me through many difficult times, 4 deaths, 4 attempted suicides, and being molested and raped as a child. This poem inspires me so much that I have passed your poem on to my thirteen year old son. And he loves it as much as I do. Thank you for such a beautiful and meaningful poem.

Jassen, Michigan

About 5 years ago I attempted suicide. I have a long history of sexual, physical, and mental abuse and decided that I did not want to live it anymore. In recovery, I was encouraged to listen to books on tape to help keep my mind on productive thoughts. I started with the 7 Habits of Highly Effective People by Steven Covey and he read your poem but did not say who the author was. The idea that others felt the same despair that I did was a revelation to me. I do believe I memorized it the first time I heard it.

Anonymous, New York

I used this poem as my competition piece in high school forensics competitions (1995-96). At that time I was significantly depressed and felt as if this was such a safe outlet for me. It turns out that at that same time, a member of our forensics team committed suicide—for all of the reasons outlined in this poem—so it also became my dedication to her. It served as my door to letting my parents know I needed to see a therapist to deal with my depression. 13 years later, I am now a Clinical Social Worker and use this poem often in my work.

Kate, Wisconsin

I first read a rendition of this poem in group therapy during a recent stay at a critical care psyche hospital. I was admitted for severe depression and a suicide attempt. My diagnosis was changed to bipolar NOS mixed, something I've suffered with unknowingly for many many years. This poem describes me to a tee, how I beg for others to keep reaching past my mask to find the real me.

Michael

I would like to thank you for actually writing this poem. The way that I came across it is as follows. I had a very traumatic thing happen to me and it has changed my life completely. I ended up getting sent to a place that helped me. One day we were in group and this poem was read. At first I didn't take it to heart. I really didn't listen when it was read, but then one day we were in group and the group was a suicide group. Your poem affected all of the people that were there differently but we all broke down in tears...Then later that day I was going through some of the papers that they had given me and I sat down and started reading the poem again and then after I read it about 5 times I realized that hey this really means something. This has helped me so much at this point in my life and even though it has many different meanings to it, it's really hit me deep in my heart and I am constantly telling people and giving them copies of it hoping that they get the same thing out of it that I have. It's changed my life.

H

I have been receiving counseling for depression after the suicide of a good friend. This has brought up other issues of loss and abandonment I had as a child. Since I went for this help I realised that I didn't know who I was. The reason? I have been wearing a mask since I was a child for protection. My counselor gave this to me and again it was by anonymous. I had to find out who had written these words which affected me so powerfully like no other written word has. These words punched through to my core and made me understand something about myself. I am glad I found you so that I can say thank you.

Jim, England

I am a post-graduate student in Plymouth, UK and came across your poem when I was undertaking a counseling course...Thank you for your gift to society. It is inspiring and captures the concepts of sociological masks to perfection, showing an understanding I didn't think possible.

Chloe, UK

My partner made me aware of this poem. She had just attended the funeral of an ex-schoolmate at which the poem had been read. The poor lady unfortunately took her own life leaving a young daughter and husband behind. I can fully understand why your wonderful poem was used. I hope it made a difference to the congregation, having just read it I can vouch it has to me. My humble thanks for enlightening a stolid old codger.

Terry

Charlie, I am 40 years old. When I was 14 years old my father committed suicide. He was a very ill man and his death was of course, tragic. It was thought by those left around to take care of me that I might consider suicide as an option to dealing with the problems in my life too (and they were many) and so I was placed in a facility that was meant to evaluate my mental health and support me and provide me with tools to ensure that I could remain healthy. It was at this facility that I first read your poem. It was shared with me by a staff member - someone who saw how desperately I was holding up my "mask," fooling everyone around me that I was just fine, that I didn't need their love and support. I never again saw these words written, until today when I googled the first line. I thought all this time that the poem had actually been written by another young person who'd been in the facility prior to my time there. I thought that only someone who'd felt the turmoil I had could have written these words. How did I forget the last few lines though? Those words are so integral to the point of the poem. I've since forgotten who showed me your poem, but the words - well, those have been ringing in my ears and through my brain intermittently for 26 years. Whenever I realize that I am once again wearing a mask, I speak the first few lines of this poem to myself... to remind myself of what I must do to get what I need in my life. AND IT WORKS.

Geri

Thanks for taking the time to let me know how and when you first ran across Please Hear, Geri. The circumstances had to have been both searing and numbing, but your spirit refused to be defeated. The empathy you gained through it all is now part of your gift to the world. That you've remembered lines from my poem all these years, and keep finding encouragement from them when you recognize the prompting to hide again behind the masks, brings me joy--and amazement that this poem I wrote almost 45 years ago keeps touching people all over the world. You're absolutely right about the last four lines being integral to the poem.

I searched the internet this morning to find and share your poem with a dear young man who has been struggling his whole life. He was bounced from foster home to foster home before coming to be part of a loving family. While seemingly well adjusted, we seem to have connected through our respective neuroses and have ongoing discussions of differences and likenesses, growing up, and how the populous relates to varying situations. While I am a childless gay man and he is a young adult straight man, he has the broad-mindedness to see beyond our innate differences and be comfortable with our friendship...I hope your poetry helps him grow through his own troubles as it has helped me with my sense of self-esteem (and thoughts of suicide so many years ago). Of course, some of the struggles remain unresolved, but the pathway was been made enormously brighter with your help.

Jim

Hello, I came to your site by chance. I was remembering my father tonight, who passed away in 1978, and thinking about a poem he gave our family one day shortly before he died. I was about 16 or 17 yrs. old at the time, and I never forgot it. I still have it, creased and tattered but still treasured. It became more valuable as I grew older and it taught me to look beneath the façade that people wear and really hear what they're not saying, to hear their heart's cry beneath their bravado. That poem was a lesson deeply ingrained because my father committed suicide shortly after he gave it to us and I wish I understood what he was saying then as I do now...I would like to thank you for becoming transparent to others so that we can see just how vulnerable we really are and hopefully use this knowledge to be a little kinder to everyone we meet.

Margaret

I'm very moved by your email, Margaret. I agree that it's the vulnerability in the poem that so many others, fearful that they battle alone, can identify with and find solace in. How hard it must have been for you all these years in the aftermath of your father's decision, wondering what might have been missed, what might have been said. I'm hoping I'm not wrong in sensing that over the years you've come to a measure of acceptance and maybe even peace with it. You've certainly found wisdom and deep empathy in your ability now to look deeper, see deeper, hear deeper, and also in your own ability to be increasingly vulnerable, as you have with me in your email. If my poem has played a role in your truly amazing journey of the heart, I can only bow down before the great mystery at work in the universe, continuously creating through each of us light where there is darkness.

I want you to know your poem Please Hear What I'm Not Saying is so true to my life. I first found this poem quite a few years back now in a psychology type book called "The Child Within," one of those self help things my mother had laying around. I read this poem daily to keep me afloat. The message touched me so much that in high school I joined the Speech Team under Poetry just so I could do your poem and get the words out to so many people. I choke up reading the words, they stab me like a knife. I have won many competitions sighting this poem and I believe it's because the message is so strong and personal to many. And how it's written, I don't think anyone could say or write it better. I have heard the anonymous version and it hasn't anything of the impact of your original. Just know you have touched at least my life and saved it as well. Though we have never met your words have kept me alive. I had a friend contact me tonight contemplating taking his own life and I tried to talk to him about it and ended up giving him this poem. I pray that it will touch him and pull him through this dreadful time. I think we are put here to make a difference and touch at least one person's life. And just so you know you have done that and so much more.

Brandy, Minnesota

I was wondering something about your brilliant poem, Please Hear What I'm Not Saying. A year ago, when I took summer school to get ahead in the ninth grade, my health class had a unit about suicide. Oddly, I found this unit fascinating, with all the psychological elements that went along with it. Your poem was passed out by my instructor, and my class and I had to decipher it. In the end, as I was told by my teacher, this poem was about suicide. Is this true? I agreed with him, but now I am questioning it. Please, if you have the time to read this and e-mail me back, I would be extremely grateful.

Katherine, California

Thanks for writing, Katherine. It's interesting to hear that my poem found its way into a class on suicide. It's been fascinating over the years to learn how many different groups of folks with various issues—for instance, addiction, PTSD, histories of abuse, etc.—have felt sure that the author must have had that particular difficulty or background in mind when writing Please Hear. But I had never heard of a connection with suicide before and would appreciate if you could let me know which lines of the poem seem to indicate that. As you may have seen on my website, I go into some detail reflecting not only on something of the history of the poem after I wrote it back in 1966 but on something of my frame of mind and intention when writing it. And as I say there I don't remember being depressed much less suicidal when writing it. That's why I'm curious to know which lines seem to indicate otherwise. Of course, when someone is playing "a desperate pretending game," that desperation could certainly lead to a sense of utter hopelessness.

My health instructor seemed so correct when he talked about it in our suicide unit, so very convincing. How odd to find that indeed he was mistaken! Maybe he corrupted my mind with bad thoughts.

As for your Health instructor being 'mistaken' or corrupting your mind, I have a different way of viewing it. He clearly is sensitized to the issue of suicide, probably especially among the young with whom he works, to the point where he devotes a whole unit to the subject in his class. A lot of people, even educators, play ostrich with their heads in the sand and avoid the subject entirely, but he knows better and is doing something about it. My hat's off to him. The fact that he was so convinced Please Hear was specifically about suicide simply means he responded deeply to the vulnerability expressed in the poem and knew where it could lead. The poem is about hope rather than despair, though, through the revelation at the end that this is every man and every woman's struggle and that there are indeed those who will hear what they're not saying, whose acceptance and love will give their hearts wings.

Chapter 10:
Out of the Mouths of Babes
(Guaranteed to Bring Smile, Touch Heart)

I'm a teacher from the Multiple Intelligence International School here in the Philippines. I have been teaching kindergarten for the past 8 years and this is the first year I was assigned to the Fourth Grade. I decided to read your poem to my class and the reactions I got were pretty astounding. I am amazed that 9 year olds actually empathized and at such a young age have felt affinity to your writing. They have experienced personal feelings of loneliness and rejection. In their own minds, they have formed a picture of you as a lonely young boy who needed a friend and they decided to reach out through letter writing. I know you had been an English teacher but I did not correct their spelling, punctuation marks and grammar as I wanted them to be able to freely express themselves without fear of being graded or marked incorrect. I hope you will take time out to read them and maybe write to us—even a generic letter to the class would be most appreciated. In the event you cannot write us back, the fact that you know your poem has reached us all the way here in the Philippines is good enough for us.

Candy, Philippines

LETTERS TO MR. CHARLES FINN FROM GRADE 4

Dear Charles

I feel sorry about no friends. Maybe that's just your imagination because you are surrounded by 20,000 guardian angels and God is your best friend.

Love, Matt

p.s. Why like very small feeble wings? You soon would get BIG heart wings.

Dear Charles,

I wonder how many masks that I use compared to you? So, if you would open yourself and show who you really are. Stop chasing dreams that are somebody else's. Your famous right? So attract more friends. Im already attracted. I accept you.

GIO

Dear Charles,

I know how you feel for I have also worn a mask. But to hide a different feeling. You are quite famous. Charles, I myself am lonely so can I be your friend. And Charles, if you want advise I say "Go for it!" Take a risk. Don't worry pal, you have many friends out there so don't hesitate to try.

Your new pal, Jolo age 9

Dear Charles,

I know that you are alone but you can make friends in different levels.

I have friends in high school but I'm only in Grade 4. See, you can also make friends.

Carla

Dear Charles,

I heard about yur letter, and I was touched when our teacher discussed about you. They say you are very famous but I haven't really heard your name-Charles Finn. I hope I can help you by the way my name is Kirk and I am 11 years old and I would love to be your friend. I will always remember your name. I hope you'll also remember mine.

From your penpal, Kirk

Dear Charles,

It's ok, I feel the same way every Friday and I'm like that too. But when you're lonely, play with your toys.

Juz

Dear Charles,

Try to find someone kind of like you then try talking to him or her. If they laugh, try walking away slowly. Then try talking to someone very kind, if they still laugh, do the same. If none of those ideas work-never give up. Those are some of the only ways to find a friend.

Sincerely, Nathan

Dear Mr. Finn,

I read your poem. I think your poem's great because I can also feel that pain. But someday, forget the past so you can take off that mask. My mother use to say to me to forget what other people think. I did that so look at me now, I'm friends with many kids. So this is what I've got next to say-everyone sometimes needs to change.

From, Chiara

Dear Mr. Charles Finn,

Mr. Finn, I know how you felt when you were writing that beautiful poem. My advice is to talk it over with someone you trust.

From Franco

p.s. I like the poem, very touching.

Dear Mr. Charles Finn,

Some day, someone will like you for who you are and you would have to take the mask off so they can see what's inside you. But be careful, some people are mean. But try your best to look for the person who sees what is inside of you.

Miggy

Dear Mr. Finn,

It is sad that you feel this way. It's okay. Everybody feels that way some time in their life. If you feel bad you shouldn't hide it. You should tell someone-it really helps you feel better. Life is very precious so do't worry, live your life how you want to.

Martina

Charles C. Finn

Dear Mr. Charles,

I read your story and you don't have any friends so I'll be your friend. I'll take the mask off.

David

Dear Mr. Finn,

In class, my teacher read out loud your poem. Here in the Philippines, I know just how you feel. In school, at recess, everybody has a buddy except me. Usually I feel lonely, well here's my advice-try not to be afraid, the worst they could do is laugh at you.

Isabella

Dear Mr. Finn,

When my teacher read your poem to the whole class, deep inside I felt very sorry for you. I felt also like I wanted to be your friend. I will give you some advice so you can have more friends. Here's my advice:
When you meet someone, be kind so he or she can accept you as a friend spend time with people you newly met. They can accept you as a friend

   That is all the advice I can give you. I hope you like my letter and I hope you follow my advice.

(No Name Given)

Dear Mr. Finn,

I really loved your story. It maid me kinda teared eye. It was really weird because I composed a song and I din't know what it really ment until I hear your poem. It really meant a lot to me. It showed me how you felt when you were writing it. It made me think about deep things. I really free. I guess we are kinda the same. Im writing this because it really

92

made me feel. Like I was floating to the sky. I also don't like hiding or any phony games. My heart also feels like growing wings. I really hope that I meet and see you.

Cody

Dear 4th Graders in the Philippines,

You guys are lucky indeed to have a teacher as sensitive and wise as you have. How happy I was to learn that she had read to you my poem and then to read your wonderful responses. She trusted that you weren't too young to think and feel things deeply, to understand that love and acceptance are stronger than the walls and masks we hide behind.

That you could feel the fear and the hope in this poem, and that some of you could identify with these feelings from your own experience, confirms the main thing I was trying to say. As one of you put it beautifully, "I guess we are kinda the same." As strong as the walls we hide behind, love is even stronger!

Never forget this, my new friends in the faraway Philippines. No matter how alone and different and unlovable at times you feel, believe that everyone else in all the world has felt this way at dark times in their lives, not only young people like yourselves but even the men and women you know and look up to, and what all of us around the world most need at such times is "the milk of human kindness" that helps our hearts grow wings! Your kind words and wise advice from half-way around our glittering Earth-home help my own heart continue to grow wings. How wonderful to discover I have new friends!

I'm reminded of a short poem by G. K. Chesterton that says it beautifully:

Once I Found a Friend

"Dear me," I said, "he was made for me."
But now I find more and more friends
who seem to have been made for me,
and more and yet more made for me.
Is it possible we were all made for each other
all over the world?

Chapter 11:
Author Clarifications and Elaborations

This poem was very inner reflective and enjoyable to read, but I sometimes felt after reading it that one is too hard on one's self and is not reflecting upon the spirit within for love and self-acceptance and being too dependent upon others for one's own self worth.

Edward, Wisconsin

Your reflection about my poem's apparent too-great dependence upon others for self-worth gets at an important point. Here are some of my own reflections 45 years after writing it. The poem's vulnerability, along with its hope, is the key, I think, to its touching so many people around the world. Some of those responding say they are either teenagers now (sometimes even younger) or were teenagers when they first ran across Please Hear. As adolescence is prevalent with identity searching and peer pressure and mask-wearing to hide the insecurity and self-doubt roiling within, it is perhaps not surprising that many in this age group resonate so deeply to the poem's candor about this deep vulnerability, and to the message of hope in the poem that they are not only not alone but that acceptance and love can yet come to help their hearts grow wings.

But many others of more advanced years, particularly when struggling with the whole gamut of physical/psychological/spiritual afflictions or addictions besetting most of us somewhere along the way, have been deeply touched and heartened by my poem, which again reassures them that they are not alone and that, thanks to the power of love to liberate them from what feels an inner prison, there is hope.

But you know, none of the above was uppermost in my mind when writing Please Hear. For one thing I was several years past adolescence at the time I wrote it (had just turned 25) and felt well grounded in early life love from my parents as well as from my Catholic faith (I was a Jesuit seminarian studying to be a priest and had just begun a three-year stint teaching in a Jesuit high school in Chicago). So I wasn't writing from great angst or depression. But even if we have been wonderfully grounded by both external love from family and friends and internal Spirit love, deep insecurity and fear remain in the background of our memory, not to mention right smack in the foreground when crises hit. One of my favorite quotes (attributed to Plato) is "be kind, for everyone you meet is fighting a hard battle." Please Hear gives a glimpse into this hard battle beneath the masks that hide it. If the battle rages less now for us than it used to, is it not because of the liberating, then fortifying, acceptance and love that we have received along the way, helping our hearts truly to grow wings? How amazed then to realize that our own acceptance and love is precisely what can help other hearts grow wings. What a force in every human life is love!

Very lovely words that inspire people. I first heard this poem on a Stephen Covey CD, where he read it. Do you really think that every man, woman and child is like that? What about the sink, the tough people that beat you up or even kill you as soon as look at you? Do you think those people are like that?

Kev

Thanks for your response, Kev. You ask a big question. Here's a stab at a response.

Please Hear gives vulnerable expression to insecurity and fear that many around the world are able to identify with, finding solace and hope that they are not alone and hanging on to the belief that love not only exists but is stronger than the strong walls they have built around themselves.

There are many, to be sure, who not only deny feelings such as these but whose behavior is so threatening and cruel (the stereotypic bully) that they're the last people in the world consciously pleading for someone to hear what they are not saying. Their walls are so thick, their hearts have been so hardened by all that they've experienced in their lives, that, hating instead of loving, it appears they are unreachable. If we believe that, we do not even try to reach. We conclude the spark has gone out, if it was even there to start with, and write them off as hopeless. But I believe there not only was a spark to start with but still exists somewhere way deep down, and, who knows, if they are not given up on they may yet feel the wind of love enough to fan that spark back alive.

I am a mother who had lost my son to adoption...It has been an excruciatingly painful journey living without him all these years, dealing with all the grief and loss and pain...But my son and I are finding our way back to who we were always meant to be. So when I read your poem I thought...surely this is written by an adoptee. It is classic identification. It speaks volumes of the inner world of an adoptee. The reason I say this is because during my healing journey, not only have I been seeking healing for myself, but seeking understanding of my son's wounded heart, how he still carries the wounded heart of the child within him, how he is very careful not to slip and appear anything less than smooth and cool, yet how he desperately needs and wants me to reach out beyond his façade of self sufficiency and to love him gently so we can tear down the walls that have been built and standing for so long...It is as though he wrote the poem himself...Know your poem will be very impacting and healing in the world of the adoptee...It is their heart's cry for sure.

Teresa

"Surely this is written by an adoptee." This calls to mind expressions from many that have read and been moved by the poem that it must have been written by a woman who has been abused, someone suicidally depressed, an agonized adolescent, one afflicted by addiction or an eating disorder, etc. That I am none of the above brings home to me the wonderful truth that when we go deeply enough into our own human vulnerability, which somehow I was able to do in Please Hear, a universal chord is struck that many others, regardless their particular struggle, can respond to. It heartens me to learn that adoptees also resonate deeply to the poem.

I was in a book store and found this book and came across your poem. It struck something inside I've never felt…it is incredible to know you can see the inside of a person when they are unable to speak. How do you know this hell I live with? Is it empathy you have that makes you know me, or is it you lived with a hell similar to mine? I don't want to be in this hell forever, it's been long enough. My therapy is getting harder and harder. These walls took 35 years to build, I'm not sure they can be truly broken down. I need someone to be my strength when I don't have it. You speak what we can never say, never tell, never mention. I know you helped a lot of people but did you live with it too?

Fran, Virginia

You ask a big question. Many people around the world, with all their different races and nationalities and personalities and life experiences, have responded over the years with "thank you for putting me into words." And that's what I hear you saying. As to how could I know you, I can only say I was giving voice to a deep part of me, intuiting at the end of my poem that I was really giving voice to a deep part of everyone. If I have empathy into others, it may be because I have listened well to myself. Because I have experienced the great good fortune to be loved, because some have really heard what I was not saying, I know for a fact that love is stronger than strong walls, and in the grace of an inspiration I found words to speak this to others. You are not really alone in this world, Fran. Never lose heart that love will reach you, and don't forget that your own love is exactly what those around you, with their own walls, secretly need. Maybe share Please Hear with some of them, and be comforted to discover that you really are not alone…I'm glad to hear that you are in counseling, and I encourage you to let your counselor know, if you haven't already, that her (or his) questions are hard and getting harder. That can help the two of you know not only the pain but the potential for "working through" the pain to a life beyond the hell and the walls. I commend you for the courage to refuse to give up on yourself and for your desire to grow.

I presented a grad presentation, as required by my school, that outlined my personality. I included your poem, Please Hear What I'm Not Saying, to have everybody understand where I was coming from. I have to say that this poem fully enveloped my personal feelings toward pretty much everybody I know. I really appreciate this poem. A lot of people came up to me after I read it and told me about how they think the same way. In addition, they said they saw me in a new light, a better light. While I was preparing for this presentation, I was really trying to find the right way to describe how I felt.Basically, I'm just trying to say that I appreciate this poem, because in no other way could I have explained in words how life was for me at my school. Thank you very much, on behalf of myself and the entire student body.

Ryan

The word that comes to mind when I think of your use of my poem in your grad presentation, and of my poem itself, is vulnerability. "Please Hear What I'm Not Saying" is not a macho declaration that "I am the master of my fate, I am the captain of my soul" but something far humbler, more honest, more human, and, yes, more vulnerable. Vulnerable comes from two Latin words meaning "able to be wounded." The more insecure we are, the more we strive to convince the world we are not insecure. The more weak we feel, the greater is our need to mask it with a show of strength. Or to say it differently, the stronger we feel about ourselves the more willing we are to take the risk to share that it has not always been so, or that the mystery of our humanity somehow blends darkness as well as light, weakness and fear as well as strength and confidence. If we lose touch with our own vulnerability, how will we respond with understanding and empathy and compassion to others who haven't yet been loved enough to discover their own inner shining, who hide their vulnerability for fear that it will be ridiculed?What I am getting at, Ryan, is it takes courage to be vulnerable as you were in your presentation. You took a risk. While I'm glad you quickly received confirmation that others could and did identify with you, and with the poem, you could just as well have received criticism or pity. You in effect did what I did going on 44 years ago when I just put

100

it out there. That many around the world keep being touched by it, and moved to share it with others as you have, says it gets at something pretty deep and real about how hungry we are for the love that is stronger than the strong walls we know so well. I have to believe that the spirit that prompted me to write what I did so long ago is pleased that you are taking the risk to pass the torch. I cheer your sensitivity and your courage.

I have felt different for so many years I can't even count anymore. I always felt hurt or rejected and still to this day take everything so personally. Never until reading this poem could I explain who I really am. I wept. I would get so angry feeling trapped with my feelings and family and friends saying "let it go," "get over it," "you have to do this." Nobody knows the real me and as I slowly try to reveal it I still feel like I get lost in translation. I have been diagnosed with OCD, post traumatic stress disorder, and bipolar II. I go to a therapist, psychiatrist, Al-anon, and I still don't know that I will ever feel like a normal person and be able to carry on. I have faked it for so many years. It almost seems easier to continue to fake it than to try and be me, because quite frankly I don't even know who that really is.

M, Illinois

Thank you for taking the time to let me know how deeply my poem has spoken to you. Perhaps sharing it with someone close will help them understand better the human being underneath those labels. I'll grant it may seem easier to try to keep faking it, but that keeps you behind those walls. May the fact that Please Hear has touched people around the world let you know that you are not alone. Never stop trusting that you will find the strength to carry on.

My name is Sarah. I just came across your quote on the internet which led me to your website. I read, saved and printed your heartwrenching poem "Please Hear What I'm Not Saying." You are very talented and I appreciate your poem, it's beautiful, you're beautiful. It's strange that I came across this because there is someone currently in my life who I believe may be the one who can help me remove my many masks (at age 28). Such a scary and palpitating thought, to let go, and become. Anyway I just wanted to say thank you. I wonder if you grew your wings...I hope so.

Sarah

Thanks for taking the time to respond, Sarah. "Ripeness is all," said one of Shakespeare's characters. That you have responded to me as you have, and are wondering if someone now in your life might help you take a risk, tells me you are ripening. Trust the process unfolding within you. Yes, I have grown wings so I know you can too. You're not alone, and you're growing stronger. Savor imminent flight!

How flattered I am that you took time to respond to me. Amazing, thank you. Truly, thank you. You said, "Trust the process unfolding within you." Your words mean so much to me in my heart, encouragement that what happens is for the good. I smile to know that you grew your wings...I appreciate your presence in my life today, a part that will always be. I will "savor imminent flight...Your quote is firmly attached to my Facebook page as I take baby steps into a new but petrifying journey.

Sarah

I first read your poem "Please Hear What I'm Not Saying" in 1991. I was participating in group therapy for rape victims. This was about my 10th attempt at finding effective therapy to overcome the trauma of being raped. I remember it was the second or third meeting, and again, I was feeling that this therapy was getting nowhere, not reaching me. But then the therapist handed a copy of your poem to each of us, and it seriously changed my life.

As we all read the poem, we all were crying, then sobbing, then hugging. I think that for many victims of rape, or violent crimes, we don't want anyone to see us vulnerable again, lest we give someone else a chance to hurt us. I was so busy protecting myself, as you say, for survival, I could not deal with the issues at hand. After this breakthrough of the group, we all managed to deal with our past, and started the road to recovery, no longer playing a victim role.

I kept my copy of your poem that I received that day, and have shared it with many friends. I am now 33 years old and a wife and mother of two great kids. Almost weekly, sometimes more often, I recall your words to help me grow as a friend, as a helping stranger, a wife, a sister, a daughter, a mother, as a person. Essentially, you have eloquently explained the phrase "It's not about me"…

I lead a high school youth group in my church, and gave them each a copy of your poem just this past Wednesday night. Everyone read a part of it aloud, and it was so powerful to hear it read among those young voices. I know it rang true for quite a few of them. I think that it broke down quite a few barriers for them…I read your poem hoping that they realize how important it is to treat each other with love, kindness, respect, gentleness, patience and mercy…

As I read your story on your website, your shock of how well traveled your poem is, how many have shared and loved it, made your poem all the more special. You didn't write it for fame or fortune, but to touch some souls. I trust you realize how many souls you have touched, and how many times, through your words, you have become an "honest-to-God-creator" of loving people.

Sandy

What a wonderfully affirming thank you with regard to Please Hear. Thank you for taking the time, Sandy, to let me know how pivotal it was not only for you but for the rape victim group years ago and then the high school youth group more recently. It reminds me of several occasions over the years when people struggling with particular issues that seem to have little relationship to each other—addicts, battered women, teenagers, near suicides to name but a few—have responded to Please Hear by saying they know it must have been written by one of them, so well did it capture something at the core of their experience. I suspect that the core experience that it did touch, and somehow give authentic expression to, has more to do with being human than any particular category...

The first time I heard this poem was in late 70's. I was unemployed mother of 3 children and in active addiction. Knowing that there was something horribly distorted in my life I was reading every self-help book that I could find and studying the Bible with a group of women. One day turning the TV to PBS and hearing Leo B. talking about his life's work and he read this poem. It touched my heart and soul. On to nurse's training and graduating in 1983, still in active addiction. I attended a workshop on stress management and "Please Hear" was in our packet. A nurse and with a new job, things should have been less chaotic, however getting worse. In 1983 I suffered legal consequences of my addiction and entered a treatment center. I have maintained continuous abstinence since that experience and often read your poem to help ground me. I am in a position at this stage in my life to be helping others through sponsorship in a 12-step fellowship and with contact with other struggling addicts. Often I bring this poem to their attention along with how I came into contact with it and how it continues to keep my self-centeredness in check. Also I have found that when I think or read this it also helps me to prevent or lift me out of the most dangerous defect of character, SELF PITY! It has also reminded me that saying "I do not know" is much easier and I consequently ask for help.

Nancy, Minnesota

Thanks for taking the time to let me know when and how my poem helped "ground" you, Nancy. Congratulations, by the way, on 24 years of sobriety! Sponsoring others now confirms for you and in you the heart of the message of Please Hear—our vulnerability allows us to connect with others for having been there, therefore for now being a wounded healer offering compassion born of understanding instead of judgment.

I know that maybe a lot of people asked you about this, but I must do that. When you were writing "Please Hear..." have you write about your feelings? Is it real, is it your experience?...Yesterday I read it first time from a long period. My attention gone to the part about second person who can bring "us" to life and that: "I fight against the very thing I cry out for. But I am told that love is stronger than strong walls and in this lies my hope." I was replacing it in my head a long time before I understood what you were writing about. And replay it now. But I'm scared to tell someone to beat down those walls.

Arnika, Poland

I appreciate your interest in my poem, Arnika, and the questions you have. There is a lovely book entitled The Velveteen Rabbit with a wonderful passage in it about becoming real—see if you can find it. It's one of those children's books that can best be appreciated by adults. When you said you're scared to tell someone to beat down those walls, why don't you give that person a copy of Please Hear to read. It could lead to sharing things at a deeper level than normal. You may even find out that person has walls up too.

Charles C. Finn

A long time ago this poem came across my desk while I was working on some taxes. I don't know to this day who brought it in. But for some reason it ended up on my desk. I read it and cried. I cried so hard that my insides were dying with every word. You see, I was sexually abused as a little girl. I grew up in a home with alcoholism, physical and emotional abuse along with it. I had a rough young adult life because I couldn't face the real me. I thought something was wrong with me. I never felt I was loved by my dad, my mom or even now my step father. So if they couldn't love me, how could anybody else, especially God, find love for me? I had to become somebody as an adult that I wasn't in order to deal with the pain and the loneliness I was feeling. It was the poem that helped me get through those days and nights of pretending. It was several more years before I was able to deal with all of the masks that I have been wearing. But I can proudly say now, that I am me now. I no longer have a mask. Although I don't have a relationship with my mom and my real dad is dead and my step is in California doing his own thing, I realize through many years of pain and tears that I couldn't choose my family. I am now helping others who are in pain to find solace in their life that was chosen for them. It has been a long road to Heaven from Hell, but I have arrived. I have been trying for years to find this poem, I finally found it!!!.

Rebecca, Oregon

Thank you for sharing with me something of the long, winding, dark and painful but ultimately beautiful journey that has led to an authentic you that no longer needs masks and pretending. You have reason to be proud of yourself, Rebecca! And that my poem in the mystery of things found its way to you and helped you through hard times to the point where you now are a lighthouse beacon of hope and solace for others going through their own hard times—well, these are truly amazing things…There is no greater joy than to realize that, not in spite of our own wounding but because of it, we can become honest-to-God channels of healing.

Having read your poem on the net one day when in a hurry, earlier in the year, and being touched by it I put it on my favourites list intending to re-read at a later date...looking through my list today I found your page again and I read it, I was touched even more deeply by its truths... How much we hide beneath our outer cover. Having spent several years in care, followed by several years of sexual abuse as a child, it took me many years to be able to feel anything like good about myself...I had survived but still felt tainted...It took me 30 years to come to terms with it, and eventually I succeeded...I'm often told how confident and bubbly a personality I have. People have been fooled by my smiles for years...only the ones who have become true friends have realized just how difficult it has been for me to overcome my past...It is the inner person not the outer cover that really matters. We all show the world only the picture we want to be seen, at first glance. It is only when we feel truly safe that we will allow others to see us as we really are, warts and all...As I read your poem I thought of how it applied to myself, and so many people I know, of how we all hide so much of ourselves for fear of being judged or perceived by others of being less than worthy... When what we should remember is that we are all "Unique." I thought of a dear friend who came to see me last night...A true friend to me, she has been my help and strength in times of need...She is one of the diamonds in my ring of life. I am sending her your poem to give her strength and reassure her that she is not alone.

Katina, South Yorkshire, England

I love your description of your friend as one of the diamonds in your ring of life and am touched that you sent her Please Hear to reassure her she's not alone. If it succeeds it will simply reinforce what she already knows from your friendship.

I was a hard headed young Marine. A pastor Named Lt. Commander Gary Robinson gave it to me. He instinctively knew I was a lost soul. And the struggles I had always had. This poem struck a cerebral cord for me. Letting me know that my struggles were "inside" myself and not unique. I felt it said what I couldn't bring my arrogant and vain self to admit to myself or proclaim to the world who knew me. It empowered me to take control of my issues. And I want to thank you and Gary Robinson for the key that started my accountability for my actions and thoughts. I'm free for the reading of this poem.

Your poem will always be the tool in which many confused, self sure, alone, arrogant, insecure, know it alls discover that their self imposed prison of anger and contempt is not exclusive. And I try and share it with anyone who I think is ready to receive the truth about themselves. Everyone without exception should experience the words you wrote about themselves. Some will "get it," some will not. Some will not let go of their deception. But I like to think the people that "get it" most viscerally are the ones who need it most.

So, when reflecting on who I have become, and aspire to be, I recognize the reading of your poem as the point in my young life that I was not alone in my paradox. Your poem was, to me, akin to my acceptance of Jesus Christ as my savior.

Ronnie, California

From a "hard-headed young Marine" and a " lost soul" you've truly come a long way, Ronnie, and to learn that Please Hear helped to empower you towards freedom reminds me of the power of words and the mystery of things.

My mother was sexually abused by her father. She was taught, "Don't think about it, it will go away." I was sexually abused by my father, and I, too, was taught, "Don't think about it, it will go away…To say we were tortured as children would be a litotes. We were abused in all the conceivable forms. Our nicest form of punishment was electric shock. We learned from the earliest possible age to never even tear up while being "disciplined." We were virtuoso with hiding any and all emotions. As I grew older, I ran from any feelings I had. When I was 20, I gave birth to a beautiful little girl. Her father was the first person I apprehensively shared this information with. I was appalled to find out 2 years later, he was sexually abusing our daughter. I felt it was a sort of confirmation of my monstrosity. I fell deeper into my "nonchalant sophisticated façade." I was lost. My sister passed your soul-stirring words on to me about 14 years ago…I couldn't believe a male had written this poem. You were the first man I had given a salutation to. Years and years of therapy later, I still turn to your words. My daughter is now 14 and is screaming "PLEASE HEAR WHAT I'M NOT SAYING!!!" Without your poem, there are times I wonder if I'd even remember what she's going through. From the very deepest, most cryptic, crevices of my heart…for my daughter, my brother, my sisters, and myself, "Thank you so much." I am going to pass your poem down to my daughter tomorrow. I hope your words console her as much as they have consoled me over the years.

Amy

I was moved that you shared with me not only at length but in painful detail something of why and how Please Hear reached into your heart and consoled you, and that you hope it might do the same for your daughter… Thank you for sharing so vulnerably, Amy. That, come to think of it, I suppose is at the heart of Please Hear's reach—its vulnerability that so many can resonate with in their own "cryptic crevices." Words from the heart carry such power.

Charles C. Finn

As an Expressive Arts Therapist who also works with Adult Survivors of Childhood Sexual Abuse, I like to focus on the image, however it's created. I encourage many disciplines especially writing even basic poetry such as acrostics. Some women find it difficult to commit their own words to a page and we encourage them to find and share any art that moves them. In two different groups I had women share your poem with their group. It spoke to them in how they show themselves in the world. They are often still using masks as they find themselves and get to know themselves. I find the poem resonates to the core of beingness. Violence, trauma, abuse aside, we all seem to struggle with presenting ourselves to the world in all our truth. We only strive for love and acceptance. We are led to believe somewhere along the way that we may not be good enough so we try to make ourselves something other so we can find love and acceptance. It seems to take a long time for us to realize that love and acceptance must come from within and once we find that, the masks can be taken off and discarded. And even along the path to healing, the masks serve us and help us to cope in many situations. There are many more ideas that come to me each time I read your poem. And I will not share them all. It seems you just got to the essence of being in the world...On behalf of all those on a healing journey I wanted to thank you for sharing.

Tammy, Ontario, Canada

What creative work you're doing, Tammy. It's fascinating to hear how you're using Please Hear in your group work and how your midwifing others along the path to healing is now finding deeper expression in your training in Shamanism. What a journey you are on!
Your observation that my poem somehow got to the essence of being in this world reminded me of some intriguing feedback I once received from a woman involved in a national (perhaps international) haiku organization and who wanted to include Please Hear in their newsletter. I was baffled at this given the succinct nature of haikus and the rambling nature of Please Hear (far longer than 17 syllables to put it mildly). Her response was similar to yours. She said just as haikus aim to hone things down to the essence, that's what Please Hear achieved, and the fact that it used a lot of words is irrelevant.

Something else you said hit home, that though the masks can eventually be taken off as bedrock self-acceptance strengthens, they have nonetheless served us well by helping us cope along the difficult way. And remembering how fiercely we used to need them can be a wonderful bridge into empathy and understanding as we hear what others are not saying and then give them the gift of discovering that they are not alone in their vulnerability, and that there is hope.

Charles C. Finn

I am presenting this poem at a local forensics competition, and I was wondering what sort of voice I should use. I have been sounding pretty angry while reading your piece, and I'm not sure what type of voice you intended it to be read with.

Deb, Virginia

I have two responses to your question, Deb. First, trust your own sense of what the poem means to you and then allow whatever voice feels right to come out.Having said that, I must admit that I've never considered it an angry poem expressing angry things. The fault is not in others for not hearing beneath my surface words of nonchalance and complacence, after all what they hear is "I'm in command and need no one." The anger might be towards myself for being too afraid to let the real me out, for fear my worst fears will be confirmed, but the tone of the poem I think is softer than that, more of a plea that someone, somewhere, somehow, will give my heart wings because, loving instead of criticizing, understanding instead of judging, she or he sees beneath my surface words, hears what I'm not saying, and gives me the love and acceptance that I hunger, that will set me free. The vulnerability in the poem would seem to call for a quiet voice daring to reveal what's behind the thousand masks.

When I found your site tonight I just had to send you an email. I have no idea if it will reach you, but I hope it does. The first time I read your poem "Please Hear" I was 15 years old and had spent my entire life up to that point living with a very sad secret. I was living in a very abusive home and was scared every day. When I read the poem I had to pause to look around and make sure no one was watching me. It scared me at first. It was as if the poem exposed my inner feelings, as if it was able to reach deep inside and read my thoughts. At the tender age of 15 I was already a master of masks. I was taught at a very young age to hide everything that I was going through and feeling from the outside world. I was told that outsiders would never understand and would most certainly turn their backs on me with disgust. Once I realized that I was safely alone after reading it, I broke down. For the first time, on paper and in black and white, my truth was there sitting in front of me. It scared me and also comforted me to know that surely I wasn't alone. For the first time I knew that there were others out there in pain and hiding too. It gave me hope! It gave me understanding! It gave me love! I never forgot the poem and could almost recite every word. I was recently trying to recall it and that's when I found your site. I wasn't going to send this message to you because I was afraid. Still I hide behind my masks. However I had no choice, I had to tell you what your words have meant for me all these years! They are a blessing to me and I know a lot of others. Thank you for sharing it all those many years ago! I've been working on removing the mask that have served to protect me since I was just a child and I think writing to you tonight is another step in that process. So, thank you again for reading this email and hearing a little of my story and what your poem has been for me. My gratitude is overflowing!

Elsa, Nevada

Had I received no other response over the years as to the impact my poem has had on hearts open to it, your response would have justified my writing it way back when. It truly touched me, reaffirming how in the mystery of things we can be heard even when we can't yet find to courage to speak. This response of yours to me, Elsa, is another step on your path of courage. My hope is that you consider taking another risk by sharing Please Hear, and its impact on you still, with someone you hold dear but with whom you haven't yet dared share this level of vulnerability. What a gift you would be giving, and I trust it will be gratefully received and will take your relationship deeper.

I can not begin to tell you how wonderful it was this morning to have a personal response from you! Thank you, so much, for taking the time. It means a lot and is a full circle moment for me to be "heard" by you…I have recently shared "Please Hear" with some very close and dear friends. It is a gift that must be shared!…I'm currently working with a very gentle and loving therapist to take the steps to remove my masks and stand in my truth and own it. It has been a long and painful journey, however I am finally beginning to feel that I am worth such an effort. I have started a book to try and help give others hope and I have no idea if I will ever have the courage to finish it and then share it and stand stripped without a mask before the entire world. I can't remember a time that I did not wear one. The healing process is long and in the end I hope to give to others the courage and the love to find their own healing.

Elsa

I love your phrase, "stand in my truth and own it." Yes! That you are getting there, and writing a book to help others discover they too are worth it, is stupendous for what it says not only about your own gathering courage but about the "very gentle and loving" counsel you are receiving. You've come a long way, girl! Long and painful journey indeed, but exceedingly worth it for the hope it can and will give others. That Please Hear gave you hope long ago blows my mind. Pass the torch, Elsa. That's what it's all about.

Your poem had been introduced to me last June by my English teacher. When he read each line to the class, he was as if reading a journal about me. Each time he uttered the words, there was like a spear piercing in my heart. The poem and me were like one. It was as if I was the person who actually wrote the poem. I show a beautiful and jolly façade to everyone, lest they know that I am but a poor, lonely and alone person. I thank you therefore for having created that poem, for it was through that poem that I discovered I wasn't the only one having this feeling... again, a million hundred folds of gratitude to you. salamat! (salamat means thank you)

Lira, Philippines

Isn't it amazing we can communicate like this, with thousands of miles between us?...Never lose heart, Lira. Learning that the façade that you wear is worn by so many others can be comforting. Remember, just as you are hopeful that others will hear what you are not saying and will give your heart wings with their love, so your own sensitivity and love is exactly what others in your life need, though they, like you, don't let on that they need it. Nothing in the world is more encouraging and freeing than love. Trust that your own heart will find wings, and that other hearts, thanks to you, will find wings. What you are experiencing now, in other words, will deepen your own capacity for empathy and compassion. Never lose heart.

I first read a shortened version of your incredible poem when I was 13 years old, and going through a very rough patch, of self-harm following the experience of being sexually abused. Whether or not you intended your poem to bring inspiration to a person in my particular situation, you most certainly did. A friend gave me a copy of your poem, begging me to read it, and after I did, incredibly, I felt understood. I had friends surrounding me who I had known for all my life, who knew me better than I knew myself, and yet it was a poem written by a stranger I had never met that made me feel the most understood. Then, last year, one of my younger friends was going through a relatively similar situation, and I gave her a full copy of your poem...She now has written a musical composition based loosely upon it, and is pulling her through her rough patch. Thank you for your amazingly perceptive poem, applicable to everyone, in every situation, just as the poem says. I still remember it, word for word, 4 years after I first read it. It has truly touched my heart.

Philippa, Wiltshire, UK

Thanks for taking the time, Philippa, to let me know how Please Hear touched your heart and helped you through a hard time ("rough patch" gives it a nice English flavor) a few years ago. I'm endlessly amazed that something I wrote for a few friends and students nearly 40 years ago has impacted so many lives around the world in the decades since, and continues to. Mysterious indeed are the ways of spirit and destiny. The credit really goes to the Spirit always on the lookout for reeds to breathe music through.

I'm a child of alcoholic and this poem shocked me when I had read it for the first time. This poem is kind of perversion, it's awful, it's so evil, scary, dreadful, terrible but it's naked truth about me. I've recently made the new Polish translation, grounded on the original text...

Blaise, Poland

Over the years a lot of people around the world have been able to identify with its "naked truth" and feel a sense of relief to realize that they are not alone, that this is not a terrible truth they need to be ashamed of but rather a universal human truth that all of us, not just children of alcoholics, experience as we work through our early insecurities, knowing that what we need most is to be loved by someone understanding enough to be able to hear what we're feeling but not saying. Maybe some of what I intended did not come through well in the Polish translation if you got a sense that I was talking about something evil or dreadful.

If I wasn't alcoholic child I wouldn't probably experience this poem as a terrible one. I mean everybody has different feelings about it and it's quite normal that same thing could be evil or dreadful for me and neutral for other person. Honestly, I was terrified by Please Hear because it exposed all my fears, weaknesses, all my pain. This poem is great and when I've written about it as dreadful or terrifying thing it was more like a figure of speech.

Blaise

Dear Mr. Finn, It is an honor to finally find out today who authored the poem "Please hear what I'm not saying." I was talking to a co-worker this morning about a poem which had so much meaning for me in the 1970's as I was a teenager growing up. She suggested I google the title and I found your website! I actually had this poem in poster form, hanging on my wall along with other "black light" posters, about 1973-1975. Between the ages of 13 and 15, I stayed in my room a lot, listening to my mother and father have their nightly yelling matches at each other. I was popular in school, always bubbly and smiling, but inside I felt weak and insecure. When I found your poem, it spoke volumes to me. I felt that someone else actually understood what I had been feeling. I would put that "Happy Mask" on for the outside world, but inside I was a hurting little girl. I made some bad choices but for the most part stayed true to myself and eventually became a police officer. I have done this job now for 29 years and your poem helped me have empathy for many people who I encounter in bad, hurtful situations. There, but for the grace of God, go I. I am still guilty of hiding my aloneness behind my mask and will probably always feel this way. Your poem reaffirmed that I am not alone in these feelings. I still look for others who pretend all is well so I can glance at them and let them know there is acceptance and love as you articulated so well. Bless you for writing this and being the voice to my feelings...I have been a police officer with Irving PD (former home of Texas Stadium-Dallas Cowboys) since 1993. I have thought of your poem often and I can tell you it was always a source of strength to me through difficult periods of my life. I was surprised to see how it has continued to touch so many lives through the years. In my profession, I have had many people tell me I'm not like most cops. That's a compliment to me because after 29 years, I still treat people with dignity and respect (until they give me a reason not to!). The words from your poem showed me we need to look below the surface of a person to truly see what's inside a person. Your words are truly a gift and I feel honored to finally meet your via internet. A grateful cop.

Naya, Texas

Thanks, Naya, for your thoughtful and affirming response. How it touches me to learn how my poem has spoken to you across your life. And how wonderful that it has helped you in your line of work to empathize with those whose hard behavior masks a very vulnerable soft interior...Dignity and respect is what people hunger for most.

I first heard about this poem one year ago at school, when my teacher had brought the book "The child within" and read this poem to the class. I was really amazed and a bit upset because I had written very similar words in my diary some time before. I immediately loved it because it dealt exactly with what I felt. Today I decided to search for information on the internet and I found this site and discovered the story of the poem. It's really wonderful…I had built heavy walls around my heart, to hide my cries and my weakness in front of other people, because I'm very proud and I don't want anyone to help me and to know how weak I am. I had also written about a mask which I wear to conceal the person I really am, because I'm afraid that the people I love wouldn't like me and would laugh at me, they wouldn't understand. Anyway, I hope, and I believe, that one day I will meet a person that will have the strength to destroy those walls and will find my heart and that secret, lonely world where I find shelter behind those walls. This is my greatest hope. These are the reasons why I immediately loved your poem. I recognize myself, my condition, in every single line.

Francesca, Italy

There's another possibility besides hoping and praying that someone some day is able to break through the walls around you and find your heart in that secret place. And that is that as your spirit self grows stronger, you will risk opening up your heart in a way that you now can't. May my poem remind you that many others—whom you would least suspect—are also hiding behind masks and walls, hoping and praying that someone (maybe you as you keep growing) has the sensitivity and strength to reach across to them. You have the power of love within you, Francesca, to free others! Trust the journey to carry you.

I've thought a lot about your words and I understand you're right. I have to try to trust people, which I seldom do, because I'm afraid they can't understand me. But I have to find the strength and the brave to open up to my closest friends at least, those who are always asking me what's wrong with me. It's not going to be simple at all. However, if I think that maybe they're hiding behind their own masks too, that I'm not the only one, this makes me feel better (the last two lines of your poem are very, very important). I want to try to help the others, if I can, with my love. Thanks for your advice. It's really precious.

Francesca

I was given the poem by my 9th grade English teacher who also happened to be the Debate and Forensics coach for the school…I learned it almost completely by heart…I've never been able to put into words how the flow of the words in that poem fits what is being said so well that it magnifies it. Even beyond the subject, it stands out as one of my absolute favorite poems…I had a friend tell me that it strongly "resonates" fortunately more with her "old self" than current.

Liz, Maryland

The comment from your friend was perceptive. While a lot of us thankfully have grown over the years past the deep insecurity and fear that Please Hear speaks to, we not only remember this old self but can relate deeply, with genuine empathy born of firsthand experience, to others still at this place of painful vulnerability. Having been there, and in some dark moments perhaps slipping back there temporarily, deepens in us the capacity, in other words, to be both understanding and compassionate. The old self doesn't so much disappear as remain embedded deep within, reminding our emerging stronger self of an earlier, more vulnerable stage in this incredible life journey.

I just reread your poem, and when I read something that I can feel is right and means something and is tuning into something, my first thought is "You nailed it!" I feel this way about only two other poems, "The World is Too Much with us" by William Wordsworth and "The Divine Ship" by Walt Whitman...I first heard "Please Hear What I'm Not Saying" as an anonymous poem presented to our Sr. Teen Group that I was in at Star Island, a religious and educational center, 10 miles off the coast of New Hampshire. Ninth grade had been difficult and Star liberated me and started me on my journey to true friendship...I just wanted to inform you that your poem had no small part in my "enlightenment" the summer between 9th and 10th grade. I think I'm still too afraid at 43 to lower my walls. I liked what you wrote about using our wounds as opportunities to make ourselves healers.

Ken, New Hampshire

Wow, to think Please Hear touched you profoundly between 9th and 10th grades. It reminds me that Black Elk had his great vision when only 9! This spirit journey is something else. It includes (thrives on, if truth be told) dark "defining moment" times...

In high school, in lieu of learning Sci-Fi, I convinced my English teacher to allow me the opportunity to study poetry. In the universe's whirling magical way, I came upon your famous poem…It was the poem I chose to learn, thus recite to the class. I did not know, back in 1976, what this poem held for me. Locked away, safely aware these words were a shield that would save me, yes, save my life. Years later, I would discover I was a multiple of mind; today they call it Dissociative Identity Disorder. My mind literally shattered to make space for all the atrocities an 8 year old girl could not handle, register, feel, as a forced member of a satanic cult. I share this because, as a non-published writer, we wonder—on those silent days of fumbling for the "it" word—do we really make a difference. I can say you certainly have in my life…The pages are yellowed, the verses underlined, parenthesis defining what I needed to learn to hear in your words kept me going. Knowing others have felt the mask of life…Knowing the Mask as okay, though mine a bit deeper in explanation, I viewed my movement through life just a Mask until I felt safe enough to allow me to be me.

Meg

"In the universe's whirling magical way"--I love it. Not that there isn't dark shattering along that way—and you've had more than your share—but how resourceful has been your spirit, Meg, to have fought through the fog of it and still found shining. That words I wrote long ago served as a shield to help keep you going brings a smile to my heart, realizing the universe's whirling magic has somehow included me. Maybe the greatest gift we can give others is to let them know they have made in our lives a difference!

Epilogue

Heartfelt responses to a message in a bottle
themselves are now cast to far shores.
In the whirling magical way of the universe,
word keeps spreading,
wings keep growing
on Earth now made safer for the heart.

In the universe's whirling magical way I came across your poem.

It is timeless. It is a view into the heart of man.

This is an extremely touching and honest poem.

Now it's like I have in words how I feel inside.

It lets me see deeply and stay true to the gold below the mask.

The idea that "mask wearing" might be universal, and not just my personal weakness/failure, was a profound paradigm shift for me.

It reminds me that there is a heart in all of us. It doesn't make me weak with rescuing everyone I meet. It empowers me with strength knowing we are all of the same make-up. In return I try to empower others with understanding.

It makes me feel at home.

It changed my perspective on the fear within me. I was not alone.

I find it extremely helpful in letting go of my anger when this person hurts me by going silent and shutting down. The poem encourages me to step back, be patient, and continue to love, gently.

It really brings to life the struggle that almost every one experiences but no one talks about.

It makes me realize I'm not alone in the journey.

It taught me how to be comfortable in my own skin.

It shows the world the silent plea of mankind.

It spoke to me about being authentic.

It gives me a new thought about courage.

It speaks directly to my heart.

It captures the complexity of human emotion. You gave us all an insight into ourselves.

I read your poem to help me accept who I am.

I find the poem resonates to the core of beingness.

I find it a gripping poem. It is so sad. Everyone should read it. There is such hope with it and yet a reality that it may never be.

There is insight in this poem. Sometimes I tell people that if you view someone through compassion or mercy, you will learn about that person.

The words from your poem showed me we need to look below the surface to truly see what's inside a person.

I had a friend contact me tonight contemplating taking his own life and I tried to talk to him about it and ended up giving him this poem. I pray that it will touch him and pull him through this dreadful time. I think we are put here to make a difference and touch at least one person's life.

It has helped me be gentler with my students and help create a safe classroom.

Every time I read it, I feel it more.

This is an incredible message. It is my story. Thank you for allowing God to use your heart.

And that is what your poem was for, to encourage us to look out for people whose "masks" hide a cry for help.

I am going through a rather difficult time in my life with somebody very close to me. You have inspired me to look beyond the "mask."

It touched my heart. Poem talks the true about us. All of us need love. But the first we must open our heart to each other and then the love is coming.

Each time he uttered the words, there was like a spear piercing in my heart. The poem and me were like one.

It opened a door to my son's soul.

It speaks to our young people and causes them to think and write.

It spoke to the kids, and to us who were dealing with them. For those of us who never walked the life of our residents, it taught them not to personalize when a kid became belligerent or angry. It made them understand that we are onions, that there are many layers to us.

I now have less fear to reach out and take a chance with others.

Obviously you have expressed a heart cry of many.

It's a comfort to feel less alone.

It portrays the importance of deep, listening relationships very well.

I thank you for my voice when I cannot speak.

To me it's a passionate love song about my life and who I am. NO ONE understands me like the poem does.

A beautiful expression from deep within the heart of all. It's not only a reminder of the pain we all feel but also how we can help each other heal.

...the subtle kindness of attitude that reveals itself, the trust in the poem.

Your poem was able to help many young people let their guard down, open up, and really talk about what was going on with them.

...your poem, an arrow to the heart...an arrow to the world.

Thank you for becoming transparent to others so that we can see just how vulnerable we really are and hopefully use this knowledge to be a little kinder to everyone we meet.

For the first time, on paper and in black and white, my truth was there sitting in front of me. It scared me and also comforted me to know that surely I wasn't alone. For the first time I knew that there were others out there in pain and hiding too. It gave me hope! It gave me understanding! It gave me love!

I read your poem to the high school youth group in my church hoping that they realize how important it is to treat each other with love, kindness, respect, gentleness, patience and mercy.

I choke up reading the words, they stab me like a knife.

It taught me to look beneath the façade that people wear and really hear what they're not saying, to hear their heart's cry beneath their bravado.

I was 13 years old, feeling very confused about who I was and feeling very alone in the world. I read this poem and realized that others felt the same way I did and that made me feel not so alone.

I read it over and over to remind me of the frailty of human suffering. It also reminds me that we all hold the wonders of hope for others needing compassion, understanding.

These words punched through to my core and made me understand something about myself.

The poem as a tool was used like a key to open the minds, hearts and souls of all who attended in preparation for the process of sharing and feedback that were to follow, so that none would think that they were any more or less secure in their humanness than the next.

I love the simplicity of it, and how it has stuck a chord with all who read it.

So many people have no idea that everyone else out there feels the same way they do. That we're all just as uncertain and unsure of ourselves as the next person. If only they could remember that, perhaps we'd treat each other a little more kindly.

Because you shared your inner most emotions with the world, people have been enabled to embrace and share the pain, express themselves better, know there are people out there just like us.

It captures the concepts of sociological masks to perfection, showing an understanding I didn't think possible.

It still continues to soften the calluses I have developed in a tough world.

My walls are still strong, but with lots of windows.

This poem is for all humanity.

It makes me appreciate my best friend even more because I thought not even she knew, but I guess she did.

It told the story of my soul as an 8th grader.

Your poem is an excellent introduction to the world of therapeutic communication

It was powerful and identified a part of my soul that was ready to be recognized and loved.

I was 15, confused about all the issues of youth, love, friendship, relationships, drugs, alcohol and what have you. I found a solace in that poem which has resonated with me so much. I have not stopped sharing it.

Every word, every line, every emotion was me. This is how I have lived my life. I am just beginning the healing journey and the road ahead is very long, but I know that I will carry this poem and its message with me until I am no more.

I will always hold onto this poem as a small treasure to offer my clients when they have difficulty finding their own words.

Your poem touches the heart and makes me much younger.

It makes relating to others quite different. Knowing they are as I am makes relating to them much easier.

The crazy thing about this poem is that soon after reading it, I found myself talking to others about it and seeing that it may have just been the thing they needed to hear, myself included. I have found that this is the paradigm in which we need to view people, from a place of nonjudgement and a place to give them a chance.

This poem touched my very soul.

It helped me seek help from others to break the walls of depression, to allow others into my life and to show emotions. Exposing my weakness helped me build my strengths again by building friendships.

As a recovering addict, it gives me a deep spiritual uplifting and reminds me to be true to self and to always remain at the service of others.

Every honest soul seeker will find something that resonates with them inside this poem.

Knowing that everyone felt that way made me able to open up and reach out to other people the way that I hoped people would reach out to me.

I have been considering divorce, but after reading this poem, I feel the renewed strength to keep trying to unconditionally love my husband and pray that I can be the one to help him remove his mask and finally let himself feel true love.

Thank you for following the leadings of your heart.

It made me think about deep things…I guess we are kinda the same…it really made me feel like I was floating to the sky…My heart also feels like growing wings. (from a 4th grader!)

It is simply beautiful how words can change a person, how they can melt a person, how they can bring hope and light to a darkened room.

It makes the world a little safer for the heart.

Appendix:
Two Related Poems

You Never Know When You Pick Up Pen

A poem I wrote decades ago
has touched many around the world for ringing true
to imprisoning fear that refuses to despair
of love's eventual freeing.
Its vulnerability diminishes as we inwardly grow stronger,
but for the sake of empathy and compassion
we'll be wise to remember.
May those still hiding behind a thousand masks
fearing the glance that knows
find comfort in learning they are far from alone
and that a saving glance is coming.
Amazing the birthing
my midwife pen was serving.

January 1988

Early Confirmation

I gave birth to a poem years ago
that continues to touch hearts around Earth
for speaking vulnerable truth about what lies behind
masks we all wear.
Metaphorically striking it rich so early
felt then a fluke but now a confirmation,
set a holy seal somehow for me
on the wholly unpredictable ritual act
of putting pen to paper.

June 1991

REFERENCE AND ACKNOWLEDGMENT

"I Want to Write Something So Simply" is found in *Evidence* by Mary Oliver, page 42, Published by Beacon Press Boston. Copyright © 2009 by Mary Oliver. Reprinted by permission of The Charlotte Sheedy Literary Agency Inc.

ABOUT THE AUTHOR

Finn spent ten years in the Society of Jesus after graduating from high school in Cincinnati. With degrees in literature and psychology from Chicago's Loyola University, he taught high school and then became a mental health counselor before relocating to Virginia with his wife in 1979. He lives near Fincastle with his family and commutes to nearby Roanoke where he is a licensed professional counselor.

Among Finn's writings is the internationally-known poem "Please Hear What I'm Not Saying." His published works, which can be obtained through his website (www.poetrybycharlescfinn.com) or e-mail address (*charlesfinn@ntelos.net*), include the following:

Circle of Grace: In Praise of Months and Seasons
Natural Highs: An Invitation to Wonder
For the Mystically Inclined
Contemplatively Sweet: Slow-Down Poems to Ponder
Earthtalks: Conjectures on the Spirit Journey
The Elixir of Air: Unguessed Gifts of Addiction
Deep Joy, Steep Challenge: 365 Poems on Parenting
Earth Brother Jesus: Musings Free of Dogma
Embraced It Will Serve You: Encounters with Death
If a Child, Why Not a Cosmos? Lovesongs to Earth and Evolution
Fuel for War: Patriotic Entrancement
Earth Pleasures: Pets, Plants, Trees and Rain
Ithaca is the Journey: A Personal Odyssey
Steppingstones to the Civil War: Slavery Integral to Each
Aging Liberal Nostalgic for Vision
Empathy is the Key: Toward a Civil War Healing
Gentle Warrior John Yungblut: Guide on the Mystic's Journey
Full Heart Singing: Letters and Poems to a Girlchild
The Mastery of the Thing! Transcendence in Counseling and Sports
Crafting Soul into Words: a Poet Sings of the Journey

All of Finn's writings relate to the spirit journey. His own has been grounded in Catholicism and nourished by Jesuit, Taoist, Native American, Creation-Centered, and Quaker spiritualities.